A MOTHER'S MANIFESTO

FINDING THE MAGIC IN MOTHERHOOD AMID RAGING HORMONES, SLEEP DEPRIVATION, AND DIAPER RASH

SARA SADIK

PARENTING BLOGGER BEHIND BYSARASADIK.COM

Skyhorse Publishing

The aim of this book is not to belittle any mama's hiccup or disregard challenges they may be facing in what is probably the most significant journey in and of their life. In fact, I am fully mindful and conscious of the struggles of many mamas and how lucky I have been to interview a few for my "every mama has a hiccup" series. They speak of their children as being resilient but the apple doesn't fall far from the tree. Let us all share more and just "be" more.

Skyhorse Publishing books may be purchased in bulk at special discounts for sales promotion, corporate gifts, fund-raising, or educational purposes. Special editions can also be created to specifications. For details, contact the Special Sales Department, Skyhorse Publishing, 307 West 36th Street, 11th Floor, New York, NY 10018 or info@skyhorsepublishing.com.

Skyhorse® and Skyhorse Publishing® are registered trademarks of Skyhorse Publishing, Inc.®, a Delaware corporation.

Visit our website at www.skyhorsepublishing.com.

10 9 8 7 6 5 4 3 2 1

Library of Congress Cataloging-in-Publication Data is available on file.

Cover design by David Ter-Avanesyan
Cover photos by GettyImages and Shutterstock

Print ISBN: 978-1-5107-6843-7
Ebook ISBN: 978-1-5107-7177-2

Printed in China

To my mama . . . because I get it now. You showed me that the hiccups are there for a reason because there would be no rainbows without them. You made me believe that I could so I would.

To my Daddy for showing me that every hardship has a lesson, a chance to succeed, and a potentially great story in it waiting to be told.

Mr. Excel for introducing me as your wife, a writer, before I believed I was one and for always putting the spotlight on what really mattered and then reminding me to jot it down on a Post-it note.

To my three little puzzle pieces for making me see the light through every crack and for making every tiny moment all that much brighter. You three make the puzzle of my heart complete.

CONTENTS

A NOTE FOR MY LiTTLE PUZZLE PiECES

Adriana (Adsi)

I wrote everything down with you and fretted and made resolutions and rice pudding. I cried just as much as you over every vaccination, if not more. I went overboard on your birthday, and sanitizing, and Gina Ford, and trips to the organic food store. I felt overwhelmed because I didn't understand that I could stay my silly self with you. Exaggerated dance moves included. You had hip dysplasia and it was then that I learned all about perseverance. I mean, why wouldn't you crawl while wearing a hip brace?

Rayan (Rio)

It's like you knew there would be one soon after you. I was chill with you and actually flew to New York when I was seven months pregnant. You forced me to see that nothing was really that big of a deal, unless it was. I was calm, cool, and collected until my water broke at thirty-six weeks. You seemed to take your time to see if you really wanted to be a part of this family, and you realized you didn't have to smile unless you wanted to. No, not even for a picture. You've got your own groove. And, yeah, there's beauty in nonconformity but you have to wear pants to school. They warned me.

Ramsey (Rambo)

I'm sorry that you were squashed in my jeans for so many days and grew in utero off the remnants of your siblings' breakfasts, lunches, and dinners. I was paranoid and extra careful with you—steroid shots and all—but survived on mostly chocolate and memories of Mykonos where you "Braxton Hicked" the night away. Well, until eleven. You taught me that I always have time for one more smile and one more dance.

A LETTER TO MY DIGITAL MAMAS

Times they are a changin' and nothing has been spared—least of all pregnancy and motherhood. I think it's great that I can order Pampers, new Havaianas, and the latest *New York Times* best-seller with one click. But our days are sprinkled with the fake . . . okay, *doused* with it. I'm swimming in it: Facebook, Instagram, Pinterest. All the time. If I'm this "taken" by the virtual, then how affected by technology will my kids be? As a mama this is and will eternally be my number one concern. Oh, that and the monumental collective panic that comes along with it. The days of buttering toast and giving it to our kids with a sore throat (something about the scratchiness helps) are long gone because our gatekeepers—anguish and anxiety—barge in with red flags about gluten, cholesterol, and crumbs.

Don't get me wrong, there are perks to being a digital mama to digital natives, I'm sure, but here are my hopes, fears, and kind requests on keeping it "real." Our kids aren't growing up like we did and there is a presumption that what was good enough for us, isn't good enough anymore. Why can't we watch *Sesame Street* and enjoy Oscar the Grouch or the Cookie Monster? The show's first five years from 1969 to 1974 now come with a warning that the content may be inappropriate for today's children. Why? Because Cookie Monster smokes a pipe, Oscar doesn't learn that happiness is a choice, and Big Bird never grows old. I don't know about you, but I'm okay with all of that. It's how I grew up, and I want my kids to experience those little bits I remember fondly with my high-pitched "Remember?" (And, yes, some of those remembers usually involved the mention of Punky Brewster and Doogie Howser.)

So, before communication is reduced to emoji-only, and I get deep into Mark Manson-esque rants in this book, here's a letter to my digital mamas. And, by letter, I mean list. Because attention spans are, well, not what they used to be. "Ohhhh, look! I got another follow and three more likes." You still with me?

1. Breathe in deep and savor the smell of crayons. No scientific journal has yet to prove that there are harmful toxins in inhaling them deeply. (Sticking them far up your nose is another matter, though.)

2. Scratch scratch 'n' sniff stickers until the tip of your finger is numb.

3. Please don't let "My battery's low" be what your little one hears you say more than "I love you."

4. Don't live your life through social media and forget that the messes and cracks are where the magic lies. Live the mess. You don't always have to record it.

5. I dare you to venture out on the other side of that glass window. Don't be afraid to get scraped knees and tousled hair from the wind. It builds character, and the scars on your elbows will make for some of the best stories and conversation starters at coffee shops or dinner parties. You know this. Don't shy away from it.

6. Having a profession is not a bad thing! Don't be intimidated by the mamas who post that they're #blessed being a mom. It's okay if sometimes you post #overit.

7. When's the last time you even saw an actual puzzle? You must think me calling my kids "puzzle pieces" is as bad as if I called them, "ma little Rubik's cubesters." Confusing and annoying as hell.

8. Will you even have the attention span to read this whole list or will you be too busy comparing baby announcements and who has a cuter Anne Geddes–style newborn photoshoot?

9. You probably stopped reading this halfway through to Google "mindfulness" and how to manage your newborn and your platform.

I think we need to be okay with not preparing our children for every possible kind of future hoping one of our efforts may pay off. We're unable to code for this, so let's all hold hands and step outside. Smile and make eye contact. Stop posting pictures of our newborns and go smell them instead. And in case you're reading this on a Kindle, at least read it with sunshine on your skin. Deal?

iNTRODUCTiON

(WOULD YOU LiKE SOME MAGiC WiTH THAT BABY, MA'AM?)

Pregnancy is a time of optimism, nausea, and relentless bouts of scrolling through Instagram wondering how those mamas appear to have it all together. There's all the other stuff, too. The hormone overload and the growing suspicions your butt will never be the same again. Impossible cravings and absurd outbursts and a busted willpower button. You overshare the latest about your bowel movements with drug store staff and ask your hairdresser for tips on how to deal with your mother-in-law (MIL), what to eat to have twins, whether or not you can still color your roots when you're six months pregnant, and if he'll come to your delivery room to give you a fresh blow dry so you look good in those first moments and thousands of pictures that capture the birth. You're as excited as a teenager with new acne medication or a millennial who's coded a new algorithm to increase organic followers: stupidly hopeful about something essentially beyond your control.

Then you become a mom. A state in which your patience and core is tested. And I mean *really* tested, as you clench your teeth and remind yourself that you really love your baby. Of course, you love them, but that poop now seeping through their onesie? That tantrum about not wanting to use the same fork for corn and chicken? Let's just say that moms, too, have a breaking point. Things aren't what you expected, nothing "snaps back into place," and you find yourself losing your phone once a day having to ask your partner to call you only to always find it in one of two places: your closet or beside the toilet.

Oh, the list of things we promised ourselves that we would never do. It's almost as long as the list we promised ourselves we would *always* do. Both need amending with this tiny footnote: Subject to moments of #parentfail. Because that happens. Not only do huge tectonic shifts happen multiple times on the baby-making ride, but these shifts bring about unplanned moments of #parent-fail. And that's okay, too. Both pregnancy and motherhood teach us how to be okay with endless chaos, hormones, and poop. It is a permanent state of frazzle. You officially have a one-way ticket to a place where the scent of sweat, tears, and mashed-up peas has replaced the heavenly fragrance of freshly shampooed hair. There are no exit visas from Mommyville, so you may as well embrace that it is far from predictable or easy, but it is also worth every doubt, tangible trepidation, and life-changing beautiful shift. It's a trifecta of accepting, adapting, and adjusting. And between these cracks lie an infinite number of silver linings, perpetual rays of sunshine, and a little bit of magic. You just have to know what to look for.

I Believe Every Uterus Is Unique . . .

Every circumstance in life hardens, softens, or defines us in some way. Motherhood elegantly does all three. If you bought this book and are not a close relative, I'd like to thank you, send you a virtual hug, and awkwardly high five you. To give you a better idea of who I am, what makes me tick, and what my pet peeves are, rather than detailing how I love spontaneity and absolutely cannot tolerate people who are rude to waiters . . . I'd like you to take a minute and close your eyes. Now, imagine that fairy godmother who knows what matters. She knows things will work out in the end even if it involves a few singing mice. (And no, *I'm* not your fairy godmother.) I'm more like the journalist interviewing her, getting it all down for you, and fact-checking her shit.

We all hit that deer-in-headlights feeling when someone asks you to "tell me about yourself." Ugh. Which is weird because I am probably one of the chattiest people you will ever meet. I'm that girl who goes into the bathroom and comes out with three new besties. I talk nonstop. About the weather. What I had for breakfast. When I last shaved my legs. What I think the couple at dinner is fighting about (and it's usually carb intake). So, yeah, I talk. All. The. Time. I'm a wife, a daughter, a sister, a crazy aunt, and a friend to even my Starbucks barista. I'm also a mama. That trumps them all.

I don't want to pretend to be an expert and I'm really not accredited or authorized to give any professional advice to anyone. I am, however, skilled in illuminating the silver linings to pregnancy and motherhood mostly through my own shortcomings and mess-ups. All from the lens of a child-at-heart, perpetual optimist, and clumsy frazzled mom. So, yes, that makes me credible, okay? Who's with me?

Why I wrote this: Partly because I longed for a voice to reassure me that packing four diaper bags full of unnecessary items the first time I left the house with my newborn was totally normal. That it was okay to jump on www.babycenter.com every time my baby sneezed. I desperately searched for the lighter side while hosting a human body and tried to tough it out by YouTubing a C-section—all while ignoring the always awkward gas. And I'm writing this from an Arab perspective since I'm half Lebanese, half Palestinian, and have 463 relatives, so you'll get to hear about the perks of that (such as having your mother-in-law visit for . . . seventeen weeks). But, I mostly wrote this because I found the journey to becoming a mama more than a little bizarre and couldn't find any literature calling it what it really is: a different time–space continuum where the only way to survive is to repeat the mantra: "It's shit now, but you'll laugh later." Where were the parenting books promising me *that*?

I want to be honest here, mama-to-be. You're about to face an uncharted journey into irrational feelings, judgment, confusion, and the sense that something else is now in control of *everything*. Yes, your partner might be supportive by casually prying that fifth cookie from your hands, but the hormones hold you hostage. From how you feel and look, to what you wear and how long you can hang around the meat section of a supermarket before you gag. (Answer: 0.9 seconds.)

So, I've tried to write the book I wanted to read when I was pregnant and during my first year in the bottomless abyss of motherhood. I wanted to read about a woman who stayed up all night panicking about her baby's twelve-week scan. You know—normal femur length, normal head circumference, and that the baby doesn't have your ears. I looked long and hard for a book about *that* mom. The one who so anxiously wants to do it all *and* look okay doing it *and* remain herself. Not so much the one who prioritizes the importance of manis and pedis, although a part of me was that mama. (I am half Lebanese, after all.) I wanted to read not so much about the mama who calls herself a hot mess and goes out to buy diapers in her slippers with a trail of vomit and merlot stains on her shirt. (Although, that's okay, too. I enjoy merlot.) More the mama who can't help freaking out about how she'll handle it: lice, vaccination shots, their eyesight, diarrhea, and, "What if I vomit when they vomit?" (The smell of my own puke makes me gag, let alone someone else's. Who cares if they started life by growing inside of me?) I was after a book about *that* mom-to-be. She's worried about all of that—the latest in the *New England Journal of Medicine*—and more. I kept looking for something honest. A book that would offer to hold my hand and tell me what so many women refuse to admit: that it's not easy. That you're *supposed* to feel lost and overwhelmed. That hating your (fill in the blank): thighs, hair, eyes, butt, mother-in-law, even partner is a basically a prerequisite to having a baby. That it's normal to want to strangle everyone who tries to touch your bump *and* everyone who doesn't try to touch your bump because that's equally as annoying. And it's fine to cringe hearing baby group moms mispronounce your kid's name for months. (Fair play because you really can't remember their kids' names, or even the moms' after five seconds.)

This is a book that says it's okay to despise almost everything about pregnancy—from ugly maternity tops to advice not to drink coffee (seriously, who follows that?)—and yet absolutely love the child growing inside you. Especially when this bump allows you to skip to the front of the snack line at the movies and gives you the last bulkhead seat on the plane. It's okay to sob, "How can I cut my eight-week-old's pinkie nail?" And normal to have no clue what you're doing 99.9 percent of the time. This includes the first time your baby poops. Or looks hungry. Or blinks.

Let me be clear, this is not a "how-to" book with bullet points of advice. There are enough of those out there. If I were to dish out advice it would be this one thing: Almost *everything* can be fixed with a catnap. And some yummy takeout. Confession: I rarely indulge in the first but love me a good kung pao shrimp takeout. I'm not here to tell you how to get your baby to sleep through the night or how to deal with your husband when he turns into a bigger baby than your newborn. Instead, this is a how-to-laugh book that focuses on the *laugh* bit of: "It's shit now, but you'll laugh later." This is a parenting manifesto that accepts the rocky road for what it is—unique to every one of us and barely manageable. And, also, a book that potentially can bring us all closer together because this book promises a toolkit of rose-colored glasses and perspective to see the whole mess—cracks and all—and how light shines through those very cracks that frustrate us in today's pressured world of perfectionism in parenting. But when we're with a non-judgmental, fun girlfriend who offers you that cup of tea/glass of white wine/shot of vodka/box of chocolates? Hell, yeah, we want to hear it all and share our secrets—the "giggle stories" and the "ugly cries."

There are many commonalities for modern moms-in-the-making across the globe. From Tokyo to Tennessee the challenges of sanitizing bottles and singing lullabies in acceptable harmonies potentially worthy for *The Voice* are the same. And, well, if you weren't too sure how to strike up a conversation with that woman you just met from Sweden or Kenya or Jordan I encourage you to mention one of two things that will turn a casual icebreaker into a lifelong friendship: husbands or mothers-in-law. Because, after all, who doesn't have a husband to bitch about and a mother-in-law to deal with?

In some strange way it might just help us cope with changes to our bodies, souls, relationships, and lifestyles if we saw someone else flailing around in desperation and struggling to get their shit together. I would love to think that I bridge differences and unite frazzled moms with my all-inclusive approach. Dare I say this could be just a tad empowering for all my worldwide readers (ummm, I do have a cousin in Senegal and another in Paris, you know!). But, then again, maybe not and maybe this book was really more for me than any of you. As a sort of therapeutic cleanse. Only, my kids are still here and in no way do I feel like I just got back from a yoga camp in Bali.

Laughter is what makes motherhood manageable. Fact. It is the pause that lets some light through. As a mom, you depend on these breaks to keep your sanity while on the hunt for that special sparkle everyone has told you motherhood is. That magic is the realization that it's okay to snort at a random stranger's advice. It's okay to lose it at your sister when she asks how little sleep you got last night. It's really okay to laugh so much you pee, and to pee so much you laugh. Every unbearable, exhausting milestone offers an opportunity to laugh at the absurdity of it all. And then we return to our lifeline, Google, for real research into what we should worry about. It's all about perspective. That is the mommyfesto. A manifesto of guidelines that proclaim there are no rules, that you have to go through it yourself and laugh and cry and google and get on with it.

As soon-to-be mamas and new mamas, we have a boatload (this is the first time I use this expression so let's applaud me on not saying "shitload" shall we?) of stuff to do. We worry and obsess and have those annoying prenatal checks and tests to show up for. But the best thing you can do right now is grab a hydrating beverage and sit down, or even snuggle with me to read (skim-reading is fine, no judgment here) *Finding the Magic in Mommyhood: How to Create the Illusion of Sanity amid Raging Hormones, Sleep Deprivation, and Diaper Rash.* Yes, it's an extended rant and mommyfesto. Yes, there's "how to" right there in the title but it's meant kinda ironically. So, let's skim-read and start some sort of a revolution or parental backlash. You deserve a pause to laugh, in advance or in retrospect of the crazy journey that pregnancy and mommyhood inflicts upon you. Your journey's been unique. Say it with me: every uterus is unique. And my unique uterus and I have loved getting this down on paper (or e-reader, or smartphone) for you and yours.

Oh, and I should clarify that I didn't write this entire book two minutes after coming home from the doctor's office with a "We're pregnant!" confirmation. I didn't even write this on day three of being at home with my newborn. Nope, I'm writing this three bambinos in. I'm writing it with a bit more composure and a hell of a lot more knowledge than the first few days of motherhood. (Okay, who am I kidding? I'm just more okay with the fact that I mess up all the time and that it's the ultimate journey of ups and downs. Motherhood really is the ultimate journey in gut management.) A lot of these sections were jotted down on my phone or on restaurant placemats or on the back of four-year-old's aquarium drawings. They were ideas scribbled down on my bathroom whiteboard mid-shower. They were typed up at night while the lull of the breast pump drowned out any chance of background silence and Zen. Little did I know that making use of the edges would allow this to happen despite the distraction the random LEGOs, birthday-party attendance pressures, stubborn stains, and efforts to wear mascara and buy more undereye concealer.

When Toni Morrison was asked how she found the time to write as a single mother, she responded that she wrote, "in the edges of the day." Honest truth? I almost let the edges slip away from me in a wave of excuses of pregnancies, hip dysplasia, breath-holding syndrome, vaccines, fevers, and all of that. Almost. Until I remembered that I just had to be ready to jump right in and catch the words. Excuse-free.

B.C.
(BEFORE CONCEPTION)

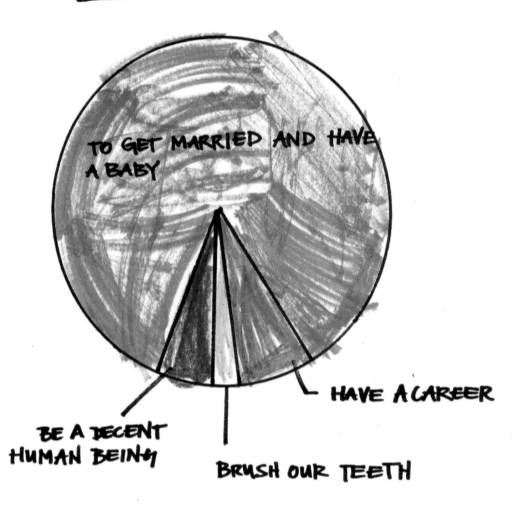

TO GET MARRIED AND HAVE A BABY

BE A DECENT HUMAN BEING

BRUSH OUR TEETH

HAVE A CAREER

1

PELVIC PRESSURE

(THAT TIME YOU MARRY THE KID YOU SAT WITH IN A TREE)

I remember loving the monkey bars. All those blisters made me feel accomplished. I was the frizzy, dark-haired girl who could barely hit the tetherball and so I would choose to swing, but not too high, with one-too-many girlfriends badly balancing on that tire swing. Sure, it was always lopsided, but that was the beauty of it. No rules, no judgment. Free play. Literally.

Playgrounds are a breeding ground of germs—like one big petri dish. I know this and you know this. But we underestimate the prophetic power they have. In a way we have conveniently brushed aside possible predictions or potential precognition of the future that playgrounds may and do show us. We bring out kids to the jungle gym when we want to sip our cappuccinos and lattes and chat with other mamas about the latest tantrum we've had to endure. (And 99.9 percent of the time, socks are at the root of all tantrums. Just FYI.) Tetherball requires a stationary pole, a rope, a ball, and some serious coordination. Awkward incoordination came easy to me, as did the fear of tipping over on the tire swing. The physical impact both these acts (and so many others) had on us as kids was obvious. Liquids were often excreted in excitement at going down a slide backwards, bones were broken trying to dodge a ball, and knees were given the opportunity to get intimate with gravel. The physical side can be healed. Cover it with a bandage, get a few stitches, and abracadabra—the boo-boo is all better.

But the playground was also where we encountered the purest form of brainwashing and inception. It was indirect which made it all the more effective. This is also why passive aggressiveness always wins an argument. DOESN'T IT? What am I talking about? Pick even the most childlike, innocent playground chant you can think of, and the odds are there's a deeply disturbing story behind it. Not convinced? Let's look at the "K-I-S-S-I-N-G" song, shall we?

After careful consideration and deconstruction, "Sa-ra and Om-ar, sitting in a tree. K-I-S-S-I-N-G" really holds a deep lyrical agenda. It doesn't work better if your names aren't two syllables. "Jane and Joe" just doesn't have the same ring. Sorry guys, but I really hope you didn't end up together. And if you did, I hope the divorce was fair and not too messy. "Sa-ra and Om-ar" is an entirely different case, however. Not only because he's a Libra and the perfect match for a volatile woman like me. So, yeah, K-I-S-S-I-N-G all the way. But then: "First comes love, second comes marriage, and third comes the baby in the baby carriage." Wait, um . . . says who? First of all, only in an *ideal* world does love turn up first. Sometimes friendship, intrigue, or even the fact that the boy or girl you like is a "giant poo-poo" overshadow any possible glimpse of love, but that wouldn't sound as sweet, now, would it? Second comes marriage. Usually, yes. But, again . . . not always. Third comes the baby in the baby carriage. What, no mention of pregnancy and days filled with white chocolate and radish cravings? And who calls it a "carriage" these days? There was my name and a boy's name and sitting in a tree and kissing and marriage and a baby. Life had been reduced to three milestones.

You may have noticed that I've put myself in that tree with a kid whose name begins with O. That's my husband. But I shall henceforth refer to him as Mr. Excel (and no, it has nothing to do with how we conceived). It's more to protect his privacy and for the purposes of not pissing him off . . . and because my parents are going to be reading this. Awkward. We met in second grade with that awful song ringing in our ears. It apparently did have quite the impression on me because we followed the lyrical instructions down to a T.

First, we fell in love somewhere on the back of his Ducati Monster on our way back from Bear Mountain in NYC. Second, we got married in Villa Accra in Ghazir, Lebanon with a duck-filled pond and a first dance to Bob Marley's "Is This Love." Yes, it *was*, Bob. *Is*, even. Third, we had a baby in a baby carriage. We actually had one, two, three babies. Our puzzle pieces. But I'm getting way ahead of myself here. Let's rewind like a VHS tape of *Full House*.

The Perfect Host

Second grade may have been the start of societal pressure to get hitched and have some "little ones," but the ball only continues rolling from there and doesn't stop. We're raised in a world in which we cave under pressure. Our teen years are intense: Have a cigarette, or an overly addictive smartphone. Have a drink. Go ahead and buy those fluorescent-colored skinny jeans. Yes, splurge on that all-plaid-and-sequined dress—it suits you. Now, I'm not saying I got married due to peer pressure. I'm just saying that women are often brainwashed to want the same things. A great man, a solid marriage (definitely better than their parents'), and a baby or three. And, of course, the ability to indulge in pizza and beer with zero repercussions regarding the state of cellulite on their ass.

Wait a second—is this why I married a big-eyed boy with a chin dimple from Mrs. Gilbert's second-grade class? Did he fall in love with me after an intense morning of coloring? I guess I really *was* good at staying inside the lines. Suddenly it all made sense. A few days before our "love affair" began (with the brief and clumsy exchange of sticky, doily-covered Valentine's Day cards we hid in our respective cubbies), some cosmic shift happened.

Eyes newly recovered from conjunctivitis . . . locked.

And so, I had met the perfect man. By "perfect" I mean that I was convinced his every flaw was *fixable* and whatever wasn't was *tolerable*. We all have preconceived notions about how our marriage proposals and weddings should be. Nothing could have been further from mine. When my husband proposed, there was no violin player or bended knee. For the nuptials, there were no Kim Kardashian–inspired fireworks or a castle waiting for me to decorate. Free from all clichés, there was a ring in a backpack, motorcycle helmets, and promises to keep things exciting . . . even at eighty.

Enter social media. Instagram, Facebook, Snapchat, Pinterest, Twitter. These platforms have really left no monumental event spared of its retouching and airbrushing and trite hashtags. They have also given us space to jump off of something into a galaxy of *"na na na na na na"* that torturous teasing jingle. But rather than going on this TEDx-ish rant of why social media is bad for us and present you with the stats, I will instead tell you that never before have I been so concerned with our futures. Remember that drug awareness campaign in the eighties? It was part of a large-scale, anti-narcotics campaign in the US where a guy holds up an egg and says, "This is your brain," before pointing to a frying pan and saying, "This is your brain on drugs." He then cracks open the egg and fries it up with a side of bacon and hash browns. Kidding about the sides, but point taken. A yummy breakfast I'm sure, but I never did drugs. Leo Burnett needs to pitch a modern campaign for social media. First shot: "This is your life." Cut to someone sitting with a cup of coffee and daydreaming. (Remember daydreaming?) The next shot should be "This is your life on social." Cue a montage of camera shots depicting short attention spans, huge waves of inadequacies, and injured index fingers from scrolling too much. Social media really skews all of our expectations. So . . . don't do drugs. Detox off social media every once in a while.

Anyhoo, suddenly, there we were, newly married and fighting (as all newlyweds do) about a long list of things. It was, and still is, the tiny things. The "ant fights," as we call them. Sure, one ant isn't annoying, but get a whole army of them and the picnic is ruined. I can never understand why he can't clear his empty coffee cup and why the *Financial Times* ends up scattered across our entire apartment and why he still reads the hard copy, but I love him for it. But, before anything came crashing down, buildings came up . . . in the desert of all places, and we ended up in Dubai. Yes, "tallest building in the world and island built in the middle of the ocean" Dubai. He was here two years before me where we endured a test of long distance, but that's an entirely different story. And maybe an entirely different book . . . a sequel? We are an international family. And by international, I mean immigrants. My dad immigrated from Palestine to Lebanon in more of a refugee way than an expat way. I've lived in five different countries, Mr. Excel's lived in four. We are so eclectic, belief-wise, nationality-wise that we celebrate everything. From Christmas to Diwali to Eid.

Living in Dubai means that I'm three hours from home: Lebanon, which was particularly accommodating as it gave me the opportunity to follow through on my occasional shrieks of, "I'm outta here!" because I could be enjoying my mom's warak enab (stuffed grape leaves) in three hours, after all. It gave me the chance to spend many weekends with my sister and her (at the time) two little boys (she now has three despite all her efforts at a strictly dairy-salt-free-stand-on-your-head diet). I was there for it all: birthdays, potty-training accidents, life-threatening jumps into the pool, and jars of glitter. Spilled over my head. I still find a few golden glistening flecks on my scalp that no amount of rigorous shampooing can eradicate. Festive at times, but mostly frustrating. Trip after trip, my sister fell into a pattern. No, not hugging me tight or crying with sadness at the thought of me living in another city. Instead, she would grip my arm and whisper in a creepy rasp to "Enjoy my free time" before having kids. I would be sitting in the Emirates airport lounge in Beirut with her advice ringing in my ears in between final calls for "Fatima Majeed," who was clearly partaking in some serious duty-free shopping.

I realized that nothing could fix this "pelvic pressure" apart from some good old-fashioned research. There was so much to do before I even *considered* sacrificing my body to another being. Like a newlywed who suddenly realizes dinner guests are about to arrive and hasn't yet figured out how to make pesto, I panicked. I wanted to be the perfect host. If little girls on the playground didn't get much say as to their future, modern society didn't realize our secret weapon: Google. I wasn't going down without proper *intel*. I'm a list girl. And a fan of the Pomodoro Technique, which is essentially a time management method developed by Francesco Cirillo in the late 1980s. The technique uses a timer to break down work into twenty-five-minute intervals with a five-minute breather. (Thank you, Wikipedia.) Basically, every headless chicken's dream because otherwise we'd be sure to waste half our day *talking* about tasks and "researching" how to focus. So, like many flights before, I spent that entire flight googling and scribbling on those sturdy paper vomit bags stashed in the seat in front. I made a list. What did I *have to do* before my life would completely and forever change—in addition to the things I knew I *should* do before getting pregnant and becoming a mom? It ended up looking like this:

1. Read the first and last chapter of *Moby Dick* so you can pretend you read it all.
2. Practice your intro dance for *The Oprah Show*. You know, for when you're famous.
3. Stop picking at your cuticles (I did not. And, yes, my four-year-old firstborn does it, too. Talk about leading or, dare I say, failing by example).

4. Marvel over the fact that you can and will order two glasses of wine midflight.

5. Take a moment and appreciate the fact that you can then pee out the wine without a strategy or logistical concern.

So, there was no denying it. The next expected step was right there waiting for us . . . like getting out of a lukewarm pool only to walk into an air-conditioned room where you freeze even in mid-July. (Also known as any mall in Dubai at any time of year.) As a couple, we had two choices: 1) continue doing what we were doing, namely screen calls (mostly from my in-laws), travel, and pretend we didn't hear the barrage of "Why aren't you pregnant yet?" queries at every wedding, funeral, and coffee run; or 2) crack under all that pressure. Before we did either, I wanted to see what all the fuss was about. Kinda like the pumpkin-spice craze that happens every October. I needed to see if it was justified. Why were people obsessing over that specific fall flavor and particular life milestone? There had to be something to it other than the sugar and the kicks. Those (sugary) kicks that have us coming back for more pumpkin spice lattes and more pregnancies. In case you missed that, I just equated a pumpkin spice latte with the miracle of birth.

Similar to the time I did a skydive, I needed to make sure of the following things: 1) I was ready—physically, mentally, and emotionally; 2) I had spoken to people who had survived before me; 3) I didn't think about the worst-case scenario; and 4) I had a farewell note—addressed to my single life, my spontaneity, and the section of my wardrobe I like to refer to as, "Can I get a free drink with that long stare?" It didn't take me long to figure out the best test to help me see if I was maternal or not was to interact with a baby. Perhaps for more than a few minutes? And no, not a random toddler in the supermarket reaching for the Froot Loops on the top shelf— that doesn't count. It just doesn't. Anyone considering parenthood should babysit a kid for a day. This should ideally be your nieces or nephews—in case you drop them, because your brother or sister have to forgive you. Don't get me wrong—it's not as if my sister left her two monkeys under my watch for the weekend. No, it was more like I was in Beirut for a few days with my husband and she happened to get an urgent work call. And they happened to have to make a poop.

Poop without Borders

It must have been March because the weather in Dubai was just starting to get hot again and the weather in Beirut was perfect. You know, the kind that calls for cute mini jackets and light dresses. Love those. It was also typical potty-training weather. It's just easier when they are half naked. You save yourself a lot of dirty laundry by hopefully catching one poop and pee in the right place. Even if the rest is, sure enough, scattered around the house like some stray puppy's work. Everyone does it (poop), but the ability to help others do it is a skill. As with all of parenting (I later found out) it takes patience and a lazy pharyngeal reflex. You basically need a bit of Zen and the ability to not have any of your five senses befriend your gag reflex.

So, Mr. Excel and I were suddenly roped into changing one diaper of poop and helping the other on the potty. "You know, to practice," my big sister laughed. (Insert eye-roll emoji here.) We thought they knew what to do. I mean, poop is poop. We expected the six-month-old to put the diaper on himself and didn't realize these two missions were harder than finding a replacement for that toy that squeals "Hello, baby lamb" before transforming into Elsa singing "Let it Grow" about her fur/coat.

The equipment required: a toilet, a changing table, and lots of reading material. They didn't know how to read, but I guess something about holding a Leslie Patricelli book was meant to relax them, get things moving, and make for some great photo ops. Check. Next thing we knew, it was full battle scene. *Braveheart* except more like Bravefart. Little did we know this whole bathroom battle required more than soap, water, and four sets of hands. Mr. Excel masked his nervousness by humming "Wake Me Up" by Avicii with the lyrics: "Feeling my way through the darkness (with lots of poop) . . . wake me up when it's all over." In his attempt to convey a relaxed demeanor he kept singing it until the boys were wiggling their butts to the beat. Okay, so that didn't happen, but it would've been nice. Then we could've flushed and sung, "Twinkle, twinkle, little star." After washing our hands, of course. After my sister's much-needed intervention, they were changed and poop-free. Okay, so we didn't wash them well, used two whole packs of baby wipes, and probably traumatized them in what should've been a totally relaxing experience. Who doesn't like taking a good poop?

While my sister was busy WhatsApping images to show her husband that we did nothing short of torture their kids, we escaped to a nearby bar. Mr. Excel brandished a shot of whiskey and started serious negotiations. "Let's make a deal that you handle all diapers and toilet stuff when we have kids." I was too busy sniffing my fingers for traces of that epic poop that I didn't answer. He apparently took that as an enthusiastic yes.

Teta's Troubleshooting

Around the time of the toilet humiliation, I fielded daily phone calls from my grandmother asking me which one of us was "broken" because the thought of planning a pregnancy or delaying it a bit in order to enjoy time with your partner and go on safaris was not something she *got*. The excuses of why we weren't pregnant grew old. I even drew up a list of possible excuses I knew I could never use.

1. We don't have time.
2. We forgot how to do it.
3. I'm rebelling against my mother-in-law's dearest wish.
4. I'm on rotation with my husband's other wives and waiting my turn.
5. I want to make sure I'm okay with our children possibly inheriting his love of bird-watching (apparently called "twitching") and awkward dance moves.

On the phone with Teta, after clarifying (yet again) that I wasn't pregnant, I would wait for the overly dramatic sigh. First the sigh, then the drawn-out silence. This was her way of telling me I was useless and lacked purpose as a wife and thus in life. All from a place of love. Her way of saying that my husband would soon divorce me if I didn't "bring for him a minimum of five boys." Hadn't she heard from my sister about our little . . . um . . . big poop run-in?

So, let me interrupt (um, myself?) and tell you I have spent a large chunk of my life being the aunt and supportive friend. I've been there for the pregnancies and early motherhood strains and sprains. I've held the end of toddler chains (always a controversial accessory . . . *are* they leashes for kids?). Well, the pressure finally got to me. Maybe it was now my turn? And more importantly, maybe we could *delegate* all the poop bits?

There was no defining moment with Céline Dion and Andrea Bocelli singing "The Prayer" in that perfect duet to accompany our decision. No uterus ribbon-cutting ceremony. No scene of dumping contraceptives down the toilet or circling calendar dates in red. I didn't go ovulation-date-obsessive. But I wanted in on reproduction. I wanted a taste of those "giggle stories." You know, the moments that moms claim make it "all worth it." The adorable things that come out of kids' mouths, their charmingly unique and extremely uncoordinated dance moves, their fashion sense when they want to get dressed, "Alooone." I knew something magical lurked in parenting. Or maybe it was an immature urge to make my own toddler crack up until they peed their pants.

Regardless, I hit up my pharmacist for the "folic" stuff and vitamins. I tried to be casual as if I were asking for a pack of gum. The problem was that the pharmacist was 1) an Egyptian gentleman and 2) a yeller. That combination made for the most indiscreet transaction ever, with him shouting from twenty feet.

"YOU WANT BREGGO TEST? YOU NEED PEE ON STICK? *MABROOK!*"

I love that he assumed I was already pregnant and congratulating me. What, no high five, Abdallah? And, anyways, I wasn't.

So, I guess the invincible forces of pelvic pressure won. With echoes of playground rhymes in my ears, like a sing-songy case of tinnitus, I shoved the folic acid in my bag. But not before a flashback to that substantial bit of poop under my thumbnail came back to me, coupled with the deafening silence of my grandmother. I knew it had to be done. Next stop: Pregnancy. It was the expected result of years of avoidance, irrational excuses, research, and also the curiosity: stuffing a pillow under my shirt to see how I would look pregnant. Not to mention all of my exaggerated moans I'd been practicing for my beautiful childbirth scene. Because I'm overly dramatic like that.

2

iNSTA-MOMMYHOOD

(THE LAND OF ENEPT)

The thing about trying to conceive is that, much like a game of Monopoly, you can't guarantee what it's going to bring out in people. For better or worse. Days quickly overflow with tantrums and irrational requests. Logic and reason are a distant blurry memory. Calendars become packed with indecipherable ovulatory notes and lunar predictions. (That folic acid can do crazy stuff to a would-be mom.)

People complicate things. We have lists on our fridges and reminders on our phones. We have notes to tell ourselves the things we need *to do* on our to-do lists. We have them numbered and scribbled down on Post-its, or in my case, on the back of my hand, like a fifth-grader. I would not be the first woman to get pregnant, so I wouldn't be the last woman to look at my husband with absolute repulsion while he slept as I tossed and turned in discomfort. I also definitely wasn't going to be the only woman to leave my phone at home to avoid my mother-in-law's thirty-nine phone calls a day. I could look ahead and confidently say passive-aggression would play a big part in my pregnancy. As soon as you decide to try and become pregnant, all of these projections and imagined scenarios start playing in your mind twenty-four seven. What kind of pregnant woman would I be? Was this something I could plan? Something I could control? Oh, God, I do not want to be like Yasmine . . . she was so . . . ugh . . . I don't know. Pregnant?

The trouble was, I'm not a planner. I'm more of a spontaneous scribbler. On the other hand, Mr. Excel swears by Excel to organize, categorize, and label everything in his life, from moving to Dubai from New York, to the suppliers at our wedding, to, of course, what to order for dinner. He's often asked, "Chinese or Sushi? Why don't we draft a quick SWOT analysis and take a moment to make the right decision?" To which I usually respond, "Ummm, baby, I don't mind what my MSG tastes like." Having said that, I'm not sure anything would get done and done *well* without this perfected skill of his. Even my own parents say I'd be homeless, foodless, and ambitionless without his contagious focus, drive, and obsessive planning. A skill I like to call ENEPT: Everything Needs Excruciating Planning & Thought.

Numbers, math, equations, calculations, and predictable certainties have never been my forte. I love words, magic, and anything with a mysterious and mystical edge. When I look at a rainbow, I see it as a beautiful spectacle of colors painted in the sky by millions of pixies. (I think my mother may have a bit of explaining to do, filling five-year-old me with pixie talk.) My husband sees it as "an optical and meteorological phenomenon that causes a spectrum of light to appear in the sky when the sun shines on droplets of moisture in the Earth's atmosphere and takes the form of a multicolored arc." Um, what? I'll stick with my pixies, thanks.

I'm a last-minute girl with lots of notebooks and faded scribbles on my hand such as: "cf de apt, org eg, and dc r dr" (confirm dentist appointment, buy organic eggs, and dry clean your red dress—*that's obvs*). Or so I *was*, until the talk of babies became less a distant thought and more of a looming event. It was only natural to imagine how the mere thought of hosting a growing baby would shake up my usual modus operandi. I had to get organized and quit the scribbles, or I'd never make a good mom, right? RIGHT? (Cue dramatic music.)

I already had a few friends who were part of the exclusive mom club. They had applied (gotten pregnant), passed (had the baby), and were now consumed by talk of baby classes, childbirth flashback stories, and their latest teething hell. I was still an outsider. I could travel on a whim and stay out until 4 a.m. if I wanted to and cure my hangover with a raw egg smoothie (I swear I know someone who does that) or burger binge. So, I decided to grab some "last-minute pre-conception reality talks." That's right, I asked moms to tell me the honest truth. I wanted a look *inside* their modus operandi. Sounds kinkier than it was.

Waah!-Waah!-Pedia

I didn't know how to prepare. Wikipedia wasn't dishing the real dirt on mommyhood, so I set up casual coffee dates and planned to *subtly* ask what babies are *really like*. I showed up with a notepad and a voice recorder. Okay, maybe not so subtle.

My first lunch was with . . . let's call her Mrs. I'm-okay-with-anything-that-happens-in-my-life-because-nothing-is-a-big-deal (and she had perfect hair to prove it). She's the mom everyone wants to be. Three kids under three. Twins in the mix yet the epitome of calm, cool, and natural. Easy to hate, except she is so damn sweet. She walked into the coffee shop with a perfect white linen shirt and didn't react to the fact that I was still in workout clothes except I hadn't worked out. Was it too early to start dressing like this? Hey, it was a Friday (the start of the week starts on Sunday here in Dubai) and I was hung over. I grabbed her arm, almost knocking off her Prada sunglasses, and whispered intensely, "We're thinking of it."

Words including *prenatal vitamins, alcohol-free, optimal weight, green juice cleanse, in bed by 8 p.m., live-in nanny,* and *prenatal yoga* cascaded from her mouth. I wolfed my not-so-baby-making-friendly pistachio madeleine, downed my scalding-hot double cappuccino, and ran off, burnt tongue thinking *I've got this.* Key takeaway: Get your shit together. If only she knew she was years ahead of Sarah Knight and had the talent to do what Knight did, which was tell me the *importance* and how-to of get(ting) my shit together. She also told me to strategize, focus, and commit while comparing me to Alvin and the Chipmunks. I'm a Simon.

So, like a typical Simon I carried on my next scheduled meeting. I met with Mrs. Life-is-hard-so-find-good-girlfriends-and-lower-expectations-because-all-husbands-are-useless-dogs. She showed up with her son and a sedated look on her face reserved for moms who have been up all night. I segued with a casual, "Soooooo babiessssss . . ." but before I could finish my sentence, she said, "Don't tell me you're pregnant." I patted my tummy and assured her that I had simply overdone the wasabi with my sushi from the night before and probably needed to start doing a few more ab workouts. Or look for the nearest bathroom.

She warned me *everything* would change. That I would hate my husband so much I'd stay up nights researching jail time for manslaughter. I kept saying, "But you're happy, right?" But she was sobbing too hard about the fact that she could hardly remember the name of her baby, let alone her address. She knew it ended with "Street" but the rest was a blank. Without her GPS, she'd be screwed.

She pushed her wrist under my nose and said "Get a whiff of what mommies smell like." Was that—sweet potato?

"That's right," she smirked, *"purée de legumes* is my new scent."

What was I jumping into? I returned to my BFF: Google, who could give me any number of moms dishing the dirt on their messy baby-filled lives. I could laugh at the mess, but where was the magic I'd heard of? Where was the damn wand?

Filters Off

Oh, social media. Oh, my dear, dear, social media. What have you done to us? To our impressions and our expectations? You've given us an entirely different vision of pregnancy, childbirth, and mommyhood. You've taken what Hollywood cooked up and micro-waved it. Don't get me wrong. I love Jennifer Lawrence, Emma Watson, Emma Stone and the gang. I really thought I could be BFFs with them at one point. Them and Michelle Williams. They all have such great hair and drive. I could picture us all leaving hilarious FaceTime Audio messages for each other or lying around getting matching temporary tattoos. That is, until I realized most roles these leading ladies play are fictitious, as are their Instagram accounts.

Let's map out the Insta-story version. The song "Hallelujah" plays in the background perfectly timed as you hold your little one's hand in yours (#blessed). I mean, really, people? Is this what was awaiting me? Heidi Klum hitting the runway six weeks after giving birth? Sure! Well, of course she did—with eight nurses and twelve trainers, wouldn't you look great too? She probably delivered in between a Bikram yoga class and boot camp. Was I going to be expected to make some sort of an appearance with oversized angel wings at my first coming-out party back belly-free? You have to love Instagram for the unnecessary pressure it puts on women, though. It really does nothing but serve up false images of what life is going to be like. We all know it, but still use it anyway. And that's another book entirely. Or TEDx talk? Or protest?

Okay, so the two women I interviewed so far had shown me different perspectives. I was confused so I did what I learned off my ENEPT husband—I made a list. It was scribbled, but full of "mom-to-be" promises to myself, my husband, and my unborn baby. It went like this:

1. I will cherish every single day of pregnancy and not use bad language.
2. I will always make all of my kids' Halloween costumes every year.
3. I will wake up and go to bed with a smile on my face because happy mama = happy baby.
4. I will never fight with my husband around my baby (unborn or born). I will speak to him in a civilized and respectful manner at all times.
5. I will not be caught dead in track pants unless I am going to or coming from the gym.
6. I will always smell nice and have my hair and nails perfectly done to keep the romance alive in my marriage.
7. Organic, baby.
8. I will only listen to music that will heighten the possibility of my baby going to Harvard. Sorry, Kanye.

I'll be revisiting this particular list later, you know, to see how I got on with these solemn vows. Suffice it to say, the Me that day, jotting down her rainbow-colored list . . . was following way too many pregnant celebrity Instagram accounts. Recipe for (say it with me), #parentfail.

Cornfields versus Ice Chips

Ah, the topic of birth itself—surely the Insta-mommyhood airbrushed deluge of fake hasn't infiltrated the big push itself, right? Birth is still messy and authentic, amiright? Let's break it down. People used to give birth in fields. Have we forgotten that? Not in private clinics with butterfly-shaped ice chips. Yes, that's right—*fields*. Where there are no guitarists to serenade you through contractions with a live acoustic version of Salt-N-Pepa's "Push It." (I'm still mad about not getting the chance to sing that as any of my babies crowned.) It wasn't so long ago that women were not blessed with the birthdate-choice-perk or safety of a C-section. They did not choose the date of their baby's birthday based on which astrological sign would be most compatible with the parents' profiles. "Virgo baby? Yes, that fits *perfectly* with a Libran daddy and Gemini mommy." Or, "We chose the birth date based on the look of the calendar date's numbers. Yes, 3-3-13 does have a magical ring to it, doesn't it?" Or how about, "We've timed the birth to be sure our obstetrician is back from his Vale ski trip. I mean, we wouldn't want him to cut his vacation short and come back all pissy at us, would we?"

So, we either have the social media-tainted version of pregnancy and mommyhood or the completely medical take on it. *Both* are inaccurate. Both are incomplete. In my pre-pregnancy reading, I noticed that the *Mayo Clinic Guide to a Healthy Pregnancy* did not mention what a screaming four-week-old might do to your sanity, your husband's hair loss, as well as your memory of why the hell you married *that* person.

I wasn't done meeting moms. I have a lot of friends. Acquaintances. People I know. People I steal experiences from. I found another mom who agreed to meet me at a new indoor play area. When we met she'd just realized her toddler's butt was leaking brown water and she'd forgotten to pack extra diapers or a change of clothes. Her eyes were glassy with sleep deprivation, yet she kept up her ironic smile, "If you want a girl you will most certainly have a boy. And vice versa. If you plan an incredible kids' birthday party, your camera will be out of battery. Everyone will be too busy for lunch on *the one* day you took more than ten minutes to get dressed and actually found your under-eye concealer." Uh, this was advice? As I listened (and watched as she fashioned a make-shift diaper out of a plastic bag and a wad of paper towels), I took a generous gulp from my cup of joe, wished it was something stronger, and got it. I would have to be ready to be tired and shameless. Hopeful and pragmatic.

The truth was squatting comfortably somewhere between the butter-fly-shaped ice chips and birthing in a field.

What I'd realized from life so far (and possibly from my Teta's drawn-out sighs and silences), was that life is not a series of perfect beginnings and endings. Life is far from a perfect Instagram post or Hollywood movie. You *will* have those moments when you get gum stuck to the bottom of your shoe, flick soy sauce on your white shirt, or have the worst hair day ever when you run into *that* ex. No rewinds, do-overs or wait-can-we-try-that-again(s). That's life. Real, messy, and filter-free.

I decided to let go of the myths and stereotypes and look forward to finding the magic in the mayhem. So, yes, at the top of my to-do list before getting pregnant was to acknowledge the beautiful force behind everything, and to be grateful we are #blessed enough to witness it. Deepak Chopra style. I could see it in that mom as she finished her iced latte while her kid played a few more minutes. I could definitely see it in the miraculous makeshift diaper that actually *contained the poop.*

I made a promise to myself to . . . contain the poop.

I promised myself to try to enjoy life the *un*-insta-stories way, hiccups and all. I hoped I could live without the glossy expectations when I did get pregnant. Doubtful, but I would try.

I was ready!

Ummm, let's see, I was *so not* ready. What was the best filter to use that would make me look like I knew what I was doing? Ahhh yes, those adorable koala ears and nose because my wrinkles and worry showed less, then.

3

OHMYGOD, ARE YOU CÓ THAI?

(SPOONING WITH MYSELF)

December in Dubai is the perfect time to stay put, although something about lying by the beach on Christmas still feels weird, so we decided to travel for New Year's. Call it an attempt at that, "Honey, the flight to Costa Rica leaves in an hour!" spontaneity or call it exactly what it was: avoiding an impending visit from the in-laws. At any rate, we booked tickets to Vietnam. When we told our families where we were going, they nodded knowingly. We didn't understand the whispers and puppy-dog stares, until it hit me. They thought we were checking out orphans to adopt. In their eyes, there couldn't possibly be any other reason to go to such a country. Tourism? No. Education on the war in Vietnam? Nope. "Why don't you go to London? Who goes to Vietnam?" they asked. *They*, meaning my in-laws. I had been on the folic acid for a month and we could say the "B" / "P" words without flinching. Vietnam was the perfect place to welcome in the New Year pre-conception and to contemplate our new aim: to get pregnant once we returned home.

Although in between touring the Mekong, renting motorcycles, and eating exotic street food, we didn't know—I'm sure you could see this coming four paragraphs ago—we'd be returning home with an extra carry-on luggage I couldn't check in. Mostly because it was the size of a grain of rice.

Let me break this down a little.

Mr. Excel is a foodie, and by foodie, I mean he needs *zero* persuasion to try anything new in any city from any restaurant regardless of how the place looks. From *oxtail amos* in Cape Town to *hormiga culona* and *cuy* in Bogotá, he'll try it. Oxtail is a kinda yummy wholesome dish until someone mentions what you're eating. Look up a picture of an ox. Now look at its tail. Yeah, so close to its butt I'm not sure that's something you should be consuming. *Hormigas culonas* translates to "ants with a large behind" (I had to google it—don't be too impressed). Salty and crunchy—like peanuts, but with a load of legs. (He didn't tell me what I was eating when I tried it.) And *cuy* is deep-fried guinea pig. Apparently, attachment to guinea pigs as pets isn't so high in Colombia. *That* I didn't try. Nor will I ever. Mr. Excel will usually finish the exotic dish and high five the cook, who always looks like he moonlights as the town plumber on Fridays. Take a minute and imagine that and the cook's dirty apron. Now, try to calm your gag reflex down. Don't get me wrong—I'm open to trying new things in new cities, but I'm not so keen on filling up my plate with anything that could be considered a pet, or brains and private parts. We have yet to visit China, but when we do, I'm not ordering the cow's vagina soup, I'm packing granola bars.

Suffice it to say, Mr. Excel and I were used to traveling without having to consider a tiny plus-one. With a mama-to-be, travel is so different because of the foodborne calamities. Pregnant women know they need to be careful to eat—if not superfoods—then at least recognizable, clean food. Uncooked items can give you toxoplasmosis or salmonella; meat needs to be well-done, and there's a big problem with sushi. Mamas-to-be really shouldn't be eating indecipherable meals in establishments where you're served by a guy with so much dirt under his nails he might have just dug his way out of jail.

I remained oblivious to the possible foodborne calamities.

There we were, carefree tourists. Pointing at pictures on menus, unable to pronounce or read a single ingredient. We hoped that our cow and chicken impersonations would be obvious enough to let them know that we were not looking to sample their lemongrass-and-coriander-infused dog tails. We turned a blind eye to the grime because this was pre-conception, right? Not week five of a baby's development.

Fast-forward to New Year's Eve.

Me: downing espresso martinis and wishing everyone a happy 2013. I made drunken promises to my husband: I would support his green cleanse smoothie initiatives (I could always pour my glass down the drain . . .), use my Kindle more (really had to find it first), stop biting my cuticles (horrible, I know), and learn how to use the Apple TV. Hey, I told you I hated technology. That's why you're reading a book I wrote and not playing some game I coded.

The next morning, I felt fuzzy and sweaty. Dizzy and annoyed. Pregnancy symptoms are easily confused with being hungover, so we didn't know that I was *có thai* ("pregnant" in Vietnamese) right away. I had clearly been hungover before, but I had never been pregnant. Here's to virgin cocktails and a new excuse to feel nauseous.

2 Percent Battery Left

I generally don't sleep a lot. There's too much to do, read, think about, munch on, contemplate, and, of course, say. In the past, I've had nicknames like Energizer Bunny, Craxi, and Pop Rocks because of my small requirement for sleep. Did you know a giraffe only needs four hours of sleep? Okay, totally random fact but good to know if I ever want to revamp my nickname to Sara the Giraffe or Gira the Saraffe. You get my point. So, I was sleeping and Mr. Excel was worrying. He later admitted he thought I had contracted some horrific virus and had to sleep it off. Either that or that all my nights of partying followed by waking up at 7 a.m. to "make the most of the day" had finally caught up with me. Either way, I was sleeping a lot. There are dozens of photos of me fast asleep throughout the trip. Pre-dinner, post dinner, at the beach, getting dressed for the beach with bikini sarong in hand, you name it, I had been caught sleeping.

I felt dizzy and generally exhausted—something I attributed to travel and Vietnamese spices. I laughed off my mom's urgings to take a pregnancy test. Moms are the most in tune with that sixth sense everyone talks about. Maybe because they're the only ones up at night to connect with it. In fact, to every photo I sent her from Vietnam, she replied, "*Habibti,* wake up, you're pregnant! I'm sure of it." Man, did she call it. Wait, did this mean we had to give our baby a Vietnamese name? I wasn't sure how my parents and in-laws would react to the prospect of their grandchild being named Hán-Nôm. I mean, you never know with all the Paris, Rome, and Brooklyn names floating around.

I'm not sure why no one admits to *trying* to get pregnant. Too much pressure or typical Middle-Eastern superstition? Nothing annoys me more than women who get pregnant "by accident." Really? By *accident*? A car rear-ending another car is an accident. A toddler potty-training who pees all over the couch constitutes an accident. But, women in their thirties with enough know-how to read a calendar? Women who have their own bank account? Women who might even know where to get the best gelato in Florence? When *those* women get pregnant "by accident," I always say, "Yeah, you mean you didn't want to have loads of conversations about 'trying'?" I can't help but think, "And how long were you on the folic acid before you had that *accident*?" Yet, there I was, accidentally with child and stuffing my face with everything including raw beef phở topped by uncooked egg. Despite being able to read, having my own bank account, and knowing where to get the best gelato in Florence, I got pregnant by accident.

"Look into My Crystal Bump"

Flying back from Vietnam, I still didn't know. It was too early and I had just *really* celebrated New Year's. Like I had crammed the past three years' worth of New Year's into one night. Cue endless guilt. I was, however, overly observant as usual (okay, stalky), as I people-watched in the airport. Or more specifically, mama stalked. As Mr. Excel chowed down on salted peanuts with his beer, I watched moms with small ones struggle onto their flights and began yet another list of "I will never, I will always." A rainbow of naive, semi-delusional promises.

There is no way to predict, and no fortune-teller can tell you *accurately*, what kind of a mom you will be. Sure, elements of your personality will creep their way into your pregnancy and motherhood. However, it is in no way a precise science of expected behavior. In fact, more often than not, the more frantic you are in life, the calmer you are in pregnancy and motherhood, or so they say. This was not the case with me. However, I have friends who were former nutjobs: always on the go, living life type-A style, planning Thanksgiving dinner in July, that had Prozac-esque pregnancies and are chill mommies. They window-shop with casual smiles even if their baby hollers in the stroller. I knew that would not be me. So, here's a quiz to shed some light on what kind of mom you might be:

1. You really think newborn babies look a lot like:
   a) Mice because of their pinkish raw texture and inability to move much. Or speak.
   b) A piece of genealogy in action, a reflection of your parents, your in-laws, and you hope they got the good bits; or
   c) Innocent, impressionable angels, a piece of heaven on earth.

2. When you receive an invitation to your best friend's two-year-old's birthday party you:
   a) Call the day after the party pretending you never got it and blame technology. That spam folder is soooo annoying.
   b) Reply you'll squeeze in an hour between your yoga class and hair appointment, as long as there's no Barney, Elmo or anything equally creepy; or
   c) Accept, mark it on all your calendars, and ask what little Adam is into these days before knowing whether or not you will have to endure a creepy Mickey Mouse, whose songs you will gladly sing along with.

3. How do you react to a crying baby on a thirteen-hour flight?
   a) Continuously huff and puff; and remind yourself to thank your husband for getting you sound-canceling Bose earphones as you blast dance remixes to drown out the wails.
   b) Let the frazzled mom hand you the baby so she can go pee, but only once (you didn't pay good money to entertain a screaming infant); or
   c) Ask to change seats to sit beside the baby. You and Tommy bond for life. You've never been a godmother before!

Mostly As: Often called unemotional, you find yourself accidentally informing children that Santa doesn't exist. You could not be further from wanting a baby. You are focused on yourself and when anyone says "bottle" you think wine, champagne, or vodka?

Mostly Bs: You are probably the type of person who orders one coffee a day, the two permissible toppings at Ben & Jerry's, and always stops at one slice of pie—even if the second is complimentary. Your mantra is there's a time and place for everything. Some find you detached. Others call you vanilla. You like to think of yourself as a realist who sees all sides to life.

Mostly Cs: You are maternal, girlfriend! If you don't have kids yet you strongly believe that it's going to be just as you expected: magical in every sense. You also still believe in the tooth fairy.

If I had known that Vietnam would not have been the ideal travel destination for me while pregnant, I would have maybe scored differently on the above quiz. Having said that, I did laugh more than usual in between the random meals where I was never sure if what we were eating was chicken or "chicken." Vietnam is also not the place to go if you're queasy, have the sense of smell of a drug-sniffing dog at El Dorado airport in Bogotá, are a picky eater, or have frizzy hair. I was all four, with a melodramatic outlook on life.

I was on a "This could be the *lasttttt* time we do (insert the activity of your choice) before we conceive" rave. This ranged from going to a romantic movie or dinner and holding hands, to sipping a fresh cup of hot coffee or walking down the street. I put the *tic* in dramatic. But still, you never *know*. This gave the vacation quite the magical air as I commented on everything with, "Ah, this could be my last hot (and carefree) latte! Amazing!"

After landing back in Dubai and to stop my mom's nonstop nagging, I paid a visit to my Egyptian buddy at the pharmacy. He hadn't dialed down on the yelling.

"YOU WANT PEE ON STICK TEST NOW?"

I nodded and bought a pregnancy test. Actually, seven.

Things were about to get real.

THE CRYMESTER

(FiRST TRiMESTER)

I've coined the following three terms: first crymester, second frymester, third buymester. They make more sense to me than this "trimester" trend. I mean, really, what use is a trimester when we are pregnant for ten months anyway? It tells you absolutely nothing of what's in store.

I wanted some detail. All moms-to-be are on the desperate hunt for those details. How much, what happens when, what fluids to expect, and above all else—what's normal?!

The first crymester is exactly what the name entails. Yup, a whole lot of crying. No, no, much more than you're imagining. I'm talking about a lot of tears. Largely without reason. Well, some with reason but no reason that can be logically justified or rationally explained.

Here's what happens: there will be an incident. Any type of incident, and you, or whoever is pregnant within a fifty-mile radius of this incident, will sob. And sob. And sniffle. And forget about why you're crying in the first place, and then vaguely remember and clutch on tight to that distant memory of why you're "upset" that it upsets you all over again. You put that memory on a pedestal and do a traditional Indian rain dance for it (of course, because it's dramatic enough and because tears are made of salt and water). So, stock up on tissues, delete any Sam Smith iTunes downloads, and make sure to warn your husband in these first few months. God help him.

CRYING DECONSTRUCTED

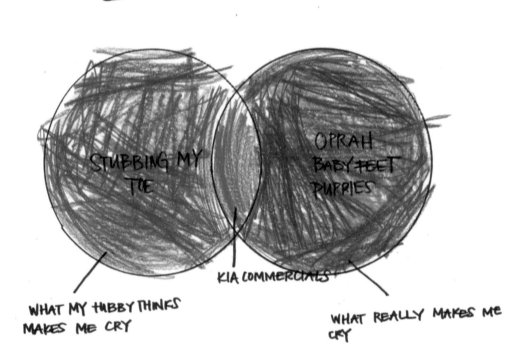

STUBBING MY
TOE

OPRAH
BABY FEET
PUPPIES

KIA COMMERCIALS

WHAT MY HUBBY THINKS
MAKES ME CRY

WHAT REALLY MAKES ME
CRY

4

TENANT OR SQUATTER

("EENiE MEENi MiiNi MO, WHERE'S MY PREGNANT MAMA GLOW?")

There is something humbling about peeing on a stick. Disgusting, actually. It sounds better than it is. You aim your stream, yet end up with pee on your hand, the toilet seat, basically everywhere *but* the stick. It's difficult to get a direct hit on that thing. Couple that with anxiety and adrenaline pumping and *voilà*! You have the longest minute of your life. You're sitting on a toilet seat with either: a) a late period, b) a missed period, or c) a baby taking over your body. Plus, in my case, the told-you-so guilt of a mom with a killer sixth sense who told me I looked pregnant way before I listened to her.

I wish I could tell you something other than what happened next but I can't: *I panicked*. The few minutes I had to wait felt like a month. I'm talking about a month at my Teta's house—the grandmother who forces you to eat chicken liver because "It's good for your skin, which always looks dry . . . like your father's." I knew that I was *supposed* to feel the beauty of this moment, but all I could think about was how many espresso martinis I drank on New Year's Eve. I couldn't stop the tears of guilt so I did what any girl would do in that situation: I sobbed to the stick. "I'm so sorry, I didn't know, but maybe the espresso cancels out the alcohol in those martinis?"

My carefree existence skidded to a halt. I went from immature thirty-two-year-old who barely reads a waiver form to skydive because she's deciding which midair acrobat move to make, to a statue—facing the most serious game changer in life.

Let me say this: although the news was unexpected it was *not* unwelcome. Yes, it would have been wonderful *not* to have eaten all of that unsanitary "chicken" and *not* be newly pregnant plus hungover, but some of the best things in life are random. Some of my most treasured memories come from events where I had no idea what would happen next—and not because I drank four glasses of white wine.

Few of life's moments can be defined as game changers. The memories stay ingrained in our minds, a permanent stamp. Kindergarten graduation (mostly for the parents and less for the five-year-old sobbing on stage, attempting to keep his cap on in a way-too-long gown) is one of them. My moment was on January 7, 2013, peeing on the stick that then determined the rest of my day, month, and next eighteen years. Unlike every other test I have taken, there was no studying I could do to truly prepare for this. Nothing. The results were there. I was pregnant. This was happening.

After a forty-five-minute sobfest with my mother who reassured me with a few lies ("*Nothing* affects the baby in the first three months!") designed to make me feel better, I contemplated how I would tell Mr. Excel. As I've been raised a believer in all religions, we open gifts to celebrate the coming of a new year in January. Get it? That means that I typically do the bulk of my shopping from December 26 to January 1. I'm not gonna lie. The sales are awesome.

I passed Mr. Excel one final present. It was wrapped in an obnoxious Louis Vuitton print and I'm sure he opened it thinking perhaps it was a pretentious (and overpriced) photo frame for his office. After he realized what it was (don't worry, I put the stick in a Ziploc bag so he didn't come in contact with my dried-up pee), he leaned in to my non-existent belly bump, yelling, "You're here? We've been waiting for you!" It was the perfect thing to say. Then, he told me he wanted to name our firstborn after his father if it was a boy, or his mother if it was a girl. Um, yeah, no. In that moment, I did what any woman would have done. I nod-shrugged and hugged him tight knowing full well that would happen over my dead body.

Guilt Expectations

I am generally a pretty private person. I like my space. I'm *also* outgoing and very much a "visual extrovert," according to the Myers–Briggs, but there's something about having your uterus taken over that throws boundaries and polite conversation out the window. Suddenly taboo topics are the norm. Mention of hair growth, urinary frequency, bowel movement irregularity, and sporadic bodily liquids that were previously never uttered, let alone discussed, become fodder for long conversations. Seconds after knowing you're pregnant, your TMI radar morphs into OMGSH (Ohmygod, Same Here!). You form friendships with strangers over mood swings, sore breasts, the fact that your saliva makes you gag, and what to do about the almost-allergic reaction you have to your mother-in-law's voice. It's all a beautiful thing.

I strongly believe that you become a mom when you're pregnant and not when you actually have the baby. And the guilt of motherhood? Well, it starts in pregnancy, when they are still on the inside. I immediately felt *so* guilty about everything: What I had eaten over the past thirty years, every point of contact with toxins—from nail polish to Brazilian blowout cream—and anything I had done that could possibly harm my precious blueberry.

I ended up with another list.

Top Six on my Guilt List (or Why I Owe My Fetus/Uterus an Apology):

1. Those espresso martinis haunted me . . . no judgment, please.
2. I ate stuff—gray-looking stuff swimming in unrecognizable white sauce. Um, pasteurized *what*? No idea what animal the meat had come from.
3. I rode on the back of a motorcycle with a large Vietnamese man who didn't understand the concept of soap—or water. Some body contact was involved. Possible transfer of something . . . ick.
4. I heard of folic acid about five minutes before becoming pregnant.
5. Superfoods, huh? Do Reese's Pieces count?
6. Kegel exercises. The only thing I'd been clenching was my jaw as I thought about who I was as a person and how I would be as a mama. Deep stuff.

At first, you can rationalize any bad behavior because, after all, you didn't know you were pregnant. You're excused, but your guilt reflex still counts all of it. And then, overnight you become one of those women who can't hug anyone who's hair is dyed or used hair spray in the last year. And forget airport security. There's a doctor's note for that. Okay, I became that woman. I may be a grown woman with an education, a few credit cards, and a valid passport, but I felt as emotionally qualified to have a baby as Lindsay Lohan. Or Chris Brown. Or Justin Bieber. Or a housewife of somewhere. The show. Not a real housewife. Anyways, my point is that the list goes on and on. I had Peter Pan Syndrome. It's a real thing. I have an inability and unwillingness to grow up and adapt to a curveball. There, I said it.

The majority of the fights between my husband and I consisted of him asking me to "be serious," and, I hate to say it, "take responsibility." I was raised by my daddy who is the funniest person I know but brainwashed us into believing that everything should be "fun, fun, fun." A hundred percent of the time. I'm not sure if it was because my father was louder (literally) in the delivery of his message than my mom or if I instinctively believed that everything *should* be fun, either way, I despise being serious. But, in my first crymester, the fact I was now carrying LIFE snapped me into serious mode.

I just wasn't sure I liked Serious Me.

Mom in the Mirror

I'm not sure if it's the novelty of the first pregnancy, the increase in serotonin, or the fact that your husband and everyone is forced to treat you like you're carrying the next Dalai Lama, but you bask in the sunshine of people talking to you in the third person right in front of you. "Oh, no—you need to cook the meat way more—she's pregnant!" Or, "Evian is the only mineral water you have? Um, remove it immediately before she empties the bottle over your head."

There was never any warning as to when I might relapse to the emotionally psychotic state of my teenage self. It could take a small trigger and there I would be hating my mom and body again with a sneaking suspicion I was missing all the best parties. I felt permanently self-conscious and unjustly treated.

Even before you hit the offensive paradox of pregnancy in which the bigger you are, the more clumsy and sweaty you become, you quickly realize there's no such thing as what to expect when you're expecting. At all. At best, it's a lot of attention and free things that people shower over you because you look so disheveled. Focus on that to get through it.

Within a fortnight of finding out I was pregnant, I straddled *these* thoughts:

1. This is not my life. Wait . . . is it?
2. Is the AC broken? Why do I still sweat even with the highest setting on?
3. I can't go out to the newest sushi place for dinner. I have to remind myself of this all the time. Where did my memory go?
4. My husband finds me scary and avoids me (and my forty-five moods) most days.
5. Is this outing worth me brushing my teeth for?

I wanted to be that adorable pregnant woman in black tights and a T-shirt that said, "Work in Progress" but I wasn't sure that was in the cards for me. And who was going to make me that T-shirt? Welcome to your crymester, the definitive sob and puke bonanza.

5

THE "MAGIC" WAND THAT GRANTS NO WISHES

(WITCH DOCTOR?)

Let's recap. And hold hands. Recording every moment? Check. Feeling emotionally vulnerable? Check. Husband asking ten times, "Wait, so up until *what* week can you travel?" Check. Puking every two seconds? Check. Peeing every three seconds? Check. Wow. I can't wait for the next seven months! Note to self: you cannot hold your pee as long as you think you can (yes, already) so go ahead and invest in a few extra dark-blue jeans. You'll thank me later.

Being pregnant is an exciting time, but the glamour soon wears off. You pee on a stick; the line is there. You pee on another stick and take a picture to send to your mom and sister and ob-gyn. Yup, it's confirmed the line is *still* there. Two lines. And just like that you're booking your first ultrasound. The heartbeat scan.

I would have loved for my mom or sister or someone from *my* side of the family to be with us for the heartbeat scan, but instead there were fifty-five members of Mr. Excel's family trying to FaceTime in. Thankfully the connection in Dubai drops frequently so it was just the two, oops, three of us.

The doctor remembered me from all of my friends' appointments. I had apparently made an impression. I decided to take it as a compliment. So, what if I sobbed uncontrollably while holding my friend's hand as she hoped for a girl after having three boys? (Who wouldn't?) I showed up for our appointment with Dr. Annie armed with notebook and pen. Dr. Annie wasn't really called Annie, but with short curly red hair, almost fake blue eyes, and dance moves on par with the movie, I couldn't help but call her that. Kidding about the dance moves, although she was hip enough that I wouldn't have put it past her. About the notebook . . . yes, it had tabs, and yes, some were highlighted. Okay, it was a binder with perfectly labeled sections and foldout flaps. What? I was named "Most Likely to Over-Organize" in junior high, you know. That had to come in handy at some point. Where are those kids that got "Most Likely to Succeed" now? I'll tell you where they are . . . reading books like *How to Teach Mandarin to Your Two-Month-Old*. Crap, I was going to have to Facebook friend them before I delivered to make it look less calculated.

So, I was happy to be sitting across from a familiar face. The same doctor most of my friends had gone to. I was hearing relatively the same information, which was comforting. Blood pressure, nutrition, multivitamins, measurements, and all the usual stuff discussed and recorded and ticked off her checklist. She had such a warm and easy tone that I wanted to ask her for that oatmeal raisin cookie recipe with crushed walnuts she must surely have. Instead, I clambered on top of her examination table cracking jokes because that's what I do when I'm nervous. Except they're not ever funny.

I doubled down on my attempts, asking if tables with stirrups like this one ever tempted couples who want to spice up their sex life. She stuck out the tip of her tongue and let out the sort of giggle you would expect a queen in the Victorian era to have. She then told me I was strong and reassured me not to be nervous. That was the best thing anyone had told me so far. Much better than my mother-in-law telling me to "eat more butter so the baby sticks."

It's at this point that moms experience their first encounter—no, not with a baby—but with *actual* motherhood. That first encounter is in its most raw form. It is primitive in nature and packaged as the most intrusive, humiliating, and inhuman of experiences.

The ultrasound wand.

Don't get me wrong, there's love here, too, in this first experience with mommyhood. But a huge chunk of the pie is made up of these cringe-inducing moments of *no privacy* where you can only hope and pray you will a) forget this very soon, b) laugh it off, c) not be so critical reviewing what went down, and d) have someone to do all three with. This carries on throughout your entire career in motherhood and it's not like any of it gets better with how high on the scale of humiliation each incident goes. There will be many so it's easier to just embrace the scale.

So, enter the ultrasound wand. (Literally, ugh.) All of a sudden, we (or me, really, it wasn't Mr. Excel's privacy breached, only mine) are in the land of ultrasound humiliation. The physical coldness of it freaked me out. This wand was not magic and I knew it would grant me precisely zero wishes. Sidenote: I wanted to call this book *Wandless* at one point. You know, mommyhood without the magic wand. And to be all cute about that ultrasound experience, but my publishers shot it down.

She went silent and I slipped further into ultrasound humiliation.

"Oh, your uterus is upside down so we cannot see. Drink water and maybe it'll reverse and we see?"

Oh, God, here we go. Immediate call to my brother who's a doctor and, okay . . . breathing again. Apparently, it's normal. He was on call and I was sorry I disturbed him at 2 a.m. but then again, I kinda wasn't because I needed him to make my heart start beating again. I resumed breathing, chugged five glasses of water, then we went back in. She still couldn't see or hear anything and Mr. Excel almost stopped breathing before she told us that she could see the sneaky baby from the inside. I remember how this early on it is sometimes difficult to detect the little one. It's uncomfortable, but it works, and we see and hear our baby!

Okay, well, the sac to be exact. At five weeks and two days there was not much to see apart from the yolk sac and so we decided to call him . . . her . . . it Gnocchi. We couldn't see much, but we could hear something. A heartbeat. *Hamdillah.*

To hear your baby's heartbeat is emotional. No jokes here. It really is a moment. Kinda like the first time you tell someone you love them. Someone other than your family members. Someone who's not conditioned and programmed to say it back. While that wand was just hanging out inside me, Mr. Excel looked for the facts. When was our due date? How healthy did the heart sound? What were the next steps? As Mr. Excel laid out a project plan (happy-stressed, but still stressed), and the nurse looked bored, I closed my eyes and meditated. Okay, that's not entirely true. I may have closed my eyes and let a tear or two sneakily appear out of the corner of my eye. Okay, I sobbed. An ugly cry.

Arab Whispers . . . Like Chinese Whispers except Nothing Like Them

I couldn't wait to call my grandma. To tell my Teta. No, not because I wanted her to hold me tight as she pet my hair and assured me what a wonderful mother I would be. Quite the opposite. I needed to call her since she'd been on my back since our wedding day about when I would be pregnant. Yes, I needed to gloat now. I mean, in between the bouts of nausea.

Arab parents are the most impatient and anxious people. This I'm sure of. It's not a bad thing, it's just, well, the way it is. Actually, let me take that back. It's not Arab parents. It's Arab mothers. And grandmothers. And aunts. And older female cousins. Basically, any Arab female in your life. But, oh, happy days. I could finally call Teta with the news.

Me: "Hi, Teta."
Teta: "Who is this?"
Me: "Who do you think this is?"
Teta: "*Habibti*, Reem!"
Me: "No, Teta, who's your favorite?"
Teta: "Tamara? No, no, Yasmine?"
Me: "No, Teta, this is daughter of Haifa and Walid."
Teta: "*Ya omri*, Mira?"
Me: "No, Teta, their *other* daughter . . . Mira's sister . . . Sara. It's Sara."
Teta: "Ohhh *ya rouhi* Saraaaa I knew itttttttt, my favorite, how are you? You sound pregnant, how far along are you?"
Me: "I AM, Teta! I'm seven weeks but shh—don't tell everyone."
Teta: "I pray you have boy. Or you will never keep your husband."

Spoiler alert: Fast-forward to birth—we had a girl. And, yes, I'm still married.

Cubicle Mom-to-Be

I kept working throughout my pregnancy . . . I hate how that sounds like an accomplishment or something. Like I need to be applauded for sitting at a desk reading the news, refreshing email inbox, and reading my daily horoscope. But, it honestly was sometimes too much—cubicle life plus growing a human in my stomach—even though my ob-gyn reminded me time and time again, pregnancy is not an illness or a disease. I feel like she would've added "get over it" to conclude her argument if she wasn't so nice.

There are, however, occupational hazards attached to working in any job while pregnant. The smells. Oh, the smells. I never thought the smell of so many perfumes fused together would make me so sick. I cannot imagine how anyone working at Sephora survives their first trimester. My office was a mix of Chanel and Dior bundled with *bakhoor* (incense burned to purify the air and deter insects and bad spirits) and, well, let's just say I'm glad I sat relatively close to the bathroom. Twelve steps to be exact. Yet, I still needed the trash can under my desk way too often. Dry heaving became my hellos. Gagging became my goodbyes.

I swore I would remain a normal woman and not enter fragile damsel-in-distress (with bump) zone. I vowed not to turn down dinners because I wanted to fall asleep at 6 p.m. I would not sacrifice style for sweatpants. I would not be the "akh woman." We all have an "akh" friend. You know who I'm talking about—the one who is six weeks pregnant and says "akh" as she bends down to tie her shoes before walking at a speed of 1.4 on the treadmill because "exercise is good for the baby." I remember seeing a pregnant mama-to-be at the office who was way past pregnant. I'm talking eleven months pregnant. And she was all up and about. I added her far-from-smooth but nevertheless persistent movements to my #pregnancygoals list.

Don't know if you're an "akh" woman? Here's a handy quiz:

1) When you found out you were pregnant did you:
   a) Immediately tweet it to the world, tagging famous idols in the hopes that they finally acknowledge you exist.
   b) Buy a baby-size pair of Converse and put them next to your husband's.
   c) Mention it in passing when sushi is suggested for dinner.

2) When ordering off a menu you:
   a) Ask for the ceviche, then smile, pat your stomach, and boom, "Oh *wait*, we can't do that now, can we?" *Wink wink.* "Just the steak very, very well-done."
   b) Order fettuccine, forget to tell them to hold the parsley, flick it off, and eat the entire dish without hesitation.
   c) Agree to a sashimi sampling menu—hey, if the Japanese do it, how can it be so bad?

3) When in a bookstore you:
   a) Ask loudly for directions to the "Impending Motherhood" section while breathing heavily to show your discomfort, then mutter, "I'm gonna need some assistance carrying things . . . I'm five weeks along . . . !"
   b) Browse the shelves, flick through two books that catch your eye before purchasing the one with the most detailed ultrasound pictures.
   c) Buy *Marathon Training for Dummies*. You're gonna have to start training, pregnant or not, when you pass the three-month mark!

4) When asked about what cravings you've been having you:
   a) Pull out a like-and-dislike chart. You have both lists on hand at all times with imagery and vocab so that you can remember forever that you could not stand the smell of celery but craved beef jerky.
   b) Dislikes are minimal and likes are maximal.
   c) You respond with "Cravings are a fabrication much like Hallmark holidays so people spend extra money and have something to talk about."

5) When poolside you:
   a) Cake on the thick white SPF 90 for fear of any sun exposure. You continuously drink water for fear of overheating and ask to move sun beds three times to avoid smoke, the smell of churros, and music—all things that make you ill because you are *pregnant*.
   b) Slap on your usual SPF 15 for that sun-kissed glow.

   c) Lather on baby oil as you sport a skimpy two-piece. Who said pregnant women shouldn't drink beer?

Mostly As: Over the top ovaries: The OMG-can-you-help-me-hold-this-paper-clip-I'm-pregnant type. She is dramatically exhausting. Yep, you're an "akh."

Mostly Bs: Chill cervix: The taking-it-in-ma-stride type. Every woman believes she is this type but statistically there is a 1.7893 in 100 percent chance of you being this chill.

Mostly Cs: Dilated denier: The what-I'm-totally-fine-of-course-I-can-trek-in-Nepal-with-you-on-spring-break-nothing-has-changed type. This type also does not exist or humankind would've failed as a species long ago.

Me? I fall somewhere between A and B. I think I'm taking it in stride, but secretly know I am not that chill. I'm convinced I'd be more stoic if I wasn't having five thousand pee breaks. Which brings me to the biggest face-off of your first trimester . . .

Cravings versus Peeing—Who Wants to Get Belly Slapped?

It's a hard call. What *is* more annoying? The cravings you can't put your finger on, or the need to urinate? Kinda like the decision you have to make when choosing which dessert to indulge in. Chocolate fondant or cheesecake? Nevermind, *that* decision is much easier. Chocolate. It's always chocolate.

You may not have a bladder like mine because every uterus is unique, remember? I know you jotted that down in your notebook of quotes to live by right under "The big secret in life is that there is no big secret." How overly profound, right? For me, peeing while pregnant composed most of my day. At first, I was paranoid that people in the office would take note of my frequent pee trips and realize I was with child, but then I remembered that I pee a lot anyway, and guess what? People usually don't notice anything their work colleagues do—unless they are pregnant and know firsthand how tiny things can become big missions. Even the most boring thing becomes a huge production as a pregnant woman . . . like going to the supermarket. If you want to torture a mama-to-be, ask them to go to the meat and cheese counter. I remember strangers gawking at me as Mr. Excel held up some turkey bacon and innocently asked, "Wouldn't that taste good in a sandwich with some mayo and roast beef and chicken breast and five types of cheese?" I couldn't answer for my dry heaving. He'd offered everything I absolutely hated in one sandwich. (Not really sure what his tactic there was.) It's hard having these symptoms in public when you don't *look* pregnant. If I was five months in and looked the part, it would be better than the stink eyes I got: "Her husband wants to make her a romantic dinner and she's gagging? What a diva!" Soon I stopped setting foot inside supermarkets and resorted to foraging like a guy in those post-apocalyptic narratives clutching a can opener in case of striking it lucky. I discovered Fun Dip with Kool-Aid–like powder and a long white stick also made out of sugar for you to dip into the sugar. Yes, sugar on sugar. Thank you, whoever invented that. You saved me from starvation.

I craved everything on the "do not eat" list. All I wanted was smoked salmon, sushi, gallons of wine, and raw veggies. I wanted street food. I wanted someone to drop something on the floor and have me brush it off on my jeans and gulp it. I wanted to be eating something and have to pull out a hair tangled from the half-chewed food in my mouth. And not my hair … Okay, maybe I would draw the line at eating other people's hair. It depended how yummy the fried takeout was. The fact that I wasn't allowed the "do not eat" food made me want it. So. Much. More. The forbidden fruit so to speak. But isn't that always the case? Pickles and yogurt. That's pretty much all I ended up digesting. And the Fun Dip craziness. Plus, *coosa bi laban* (zucchini stuffed with rice, meat, and pine nuts in yogurt). Olives, cottage cheese, cashews. All wolfed down. Can I just say that pickles and pregnant women thing is not a myth? There's something about that sour crunch.

But the most annoying thing about cravings?

They change every two seconds, and I don't mean from a spicy penne dish to ravioli. No, I'm saying you want fish curry until it shows up, when you decide you want, no, NEED a bit of spicy chicken. You would kill for it. And if that wasn't enough, cravings seem to be personality linked. So, the bigger the drama queen you are the more stable your cravings are, the healthier you are the unhealthier your cravings are, and the more independent you are the more childlike you become. Take grilled cheese on toast. You'll totally go there even though you left home at seventeen and became a professional chef. Just go with it. Go with it all. The empty cartons of Ben & Jerry's. The prawn-flavored crisps for breakfast. The most orange mac and cheese and that margherita pizza when you desperately want a margarita. Whatever stays down gets a thumbs-up.

I craved different things with all three pregnancies, though. My first? Curry. Chicken tikka, chicken tikka masala, chicken korma, aloo gobi, biryani rice, and the spicier the better, really. No wonder she was born without hair. (Sorry 'bout that, little gnocchi.) My craving for Indian food was easily satisfied because a good curry is easy to find in Dubai. I only ate fish with my second, and crumbs and scraps with my third. Maybe that's why my second is so picky and my third . . . well, let's just say my problem with him is definitely not feeding him. You know, mostly because he believes he's entitled to three meals a day. And by that, I mean three breakfasts, three lunches, and three dinners. When does it stop being baby fat again?

Anyway, back to getting through the first crymester.

Here are my top tips for your partner to get you through—because, remember, it's called the crymester for a reason. And because they deserve to read at least one page of this book. (Okay, two. They have a special quiz to read right before birth, too.)

- Compliment your wife. Twice a day, daily. (Yes, lip mustaches can be attractive.) From now on until, well, forever, your wife—the bearer of your unborn child—is all you have eyes for. You find her destroyed navel and stretch marks unbelievably sexy. And that extra chin hair? Offers to braid that will be richly rewarded.
- Don't even think about trying to win an argument. She's carrying your child . . . inside her. She wins.
- Do not disregard the urgency to pee. It's much easier to take five minutes to pull over on the side of the road than to try and wipe down car seats. You'll have to do that soon enough for your toddlers when they're potty training.

- Don't deny cravings. Your logic will not convince her that she doesn't need cream-cheese-filled wontons with lemon ice cream at 3 a.m. Nobody will "thank you later." Hand it over or be prepared for Pregzilla as she murmurs "Outta my way or I will belly slap you."

6

THE ULTIMATE CARTE BLANCHE

(CELEBRITY TWINS AND DUFBL)

At this stage you may still be puking and unable to bear the smell of your husband. But take heart, there is stuff you can get away with as a pregnant woman. It's time you embrace some amazing new skills. Meet your new self. She has a whole new level of vagueness. It's her prerogative to stand in the fresh produce section with an empty basket staring intently at the rows of breakfast cereals wondering what on earth she's there to buy. Finally, she makes a decision—only to buy a new kettle, some dried mango, and two packets of spinach. But, wait, she can't go home because she left her keys inside the fresh OJ machine. And her phone's in with the frozen pizzas.

And so begins your DUFBL period. It's like Picasso's Blue Period except much more socially unaccepted. DUFBL stands for: Ditzy, Unbelievably Flaky, Bad Listener. You know, someone just like me. And you now. Here's how she rolls:

You: "Should I go to that dinner party tonight?"
Ditzy: "That was tonight? I wrote it down as next month."
Unbelievably Flaky: "I'm going to confirm, then not show up."
Bad Listener: "Who?"

Ah, but another perk of being pregnant is your new twin bestie. You've always wanted to have a twin, and now you get to have one. And no, not as in you find a lump in your neck, get it checked, and they tell you it's actually a clump of hair and a few fingernails.

Yes, exactly like that scene in *My Big Fat Greek Wedding*. Gross. No, I'm talking about your pregnant celebrity twin. Everyone has one. A celebrity who's due around the same time as you (except she has dozens of stylists getting her look together every morning and someone to brush her teeth for her while she snoozes an extra five minutes).

How do you find yours? Social media, baby. Where else?

My celebrity twin was Kate Middleton expecting Prince George. Kim Kardashian would have been less pressure—I mean, honestly, the future Queen of the United Kingdom and the Commonwealth having her first child while I expected mine? That's pressure. As Kate's pregnancy progressed and she remained a fashion icon with dress designs that sold out in minutes while mine got stained in minutes, I got competitive. I descended into self-criticism and wondered if she, too, was pulling out random gray hairs in anticipation of being responsible for a whole other person. I'm talking a whole entire person who will poop and fall in love, eat pizza, and parallel park badly—and not necessarily in that order.

My advice? It's best to scrutinize your celebrity twin, while keeping your view of your own body's changes strictly in la-la land. Try not to make eye contact with yourself in the mirror as your navel shreds into an unrecognizable smear and you grow hair in new places. Ignore the potential of stretch marks and persistent cellulite. I'm sure Kate did, too. It's all just easier that way. And do not listen to older female relatives who push food on you and encourage you to wear a tent. Those angles can and will be hidden by a filter and photoshopped or you can just go ahead and continue taking pictures of your bump and feet and those original tiles. Don't forget to hashtag blessed.

I realized early on that we all need a few real-life besties to get us through these DUFBL days and the celebrity stalking. Preferably someone who's been married the exact same number of days as you. If you are on the hunt for a new bestie, be aware the criteria's totally changed.

Pre-kids, your bestie will:

1. Think you trying to stuff thirty-five cherries in your mouth and then reading the news is hilarious.
2. Like eighties and R & B music so no fighting over what club to go out to.
3. Order your dirty martini—extra dirty—while you take a trip to the restroom.

4. Listen to you talk about a boy you met once who you are convinced likes you because he blinked in your general direction . . . flirtatiously.
5. Be patient when she can't hear you over the loud music when you're trying to tell her whose name the table is under after three failed texts.

Post-kids, your bestie will:

1. Study your WhatsApp image carefully enough to tell you if your baby's poop looks "normal."
2. Listen to you cry about how tired you are and not try to 'fix it' but instead, simply make eye contact and say, "I know . . ." much unlike your husband.
3. Get your soy iced pumpkin spice coffee order right before you get there.
4. Listen to you say, "I'm going to have a breakdown" and let you have one, or better yet, have one with you.
5. Be patient when she can't hear you over your two-year-old's screams while you wash the kid's hair.

At the end of the day, if you can't share some exhausted, parenting-fail confession with your girlfriend and receive a simple, "I've done that, too," there's always the Delete Contact option. Or you can keep sending her the photos of baby poop until she ups her game. Having that bestie by your side is even more important than having her at your wedding day when she was in charge of calming everyone the f down. Oh, and by everyone, I mean your mom and his. She will nod in confirmation when you tell people how much you're peeing and get teary-eyed with you when you're honest about being scared of having a C-section. So, choose wisely who you want watching that whole show going down and who will put up with your personality changing 180 degrees every five minutes.

When to Tell People You Are Pregnant

When is it a good time to share the news it's a baby and not a burger in there? There is no perfect time to share your news because their reaction will never be as big as you secretly hope it will be. Just saying. Get used to that. You will hype it up in your head and, well . . . for them? For them it's just another woman who's about to balloon and enter the strange alternate universe of mentioning her kids and husband and weird diaper rash and breast milk into every conversation. Like I did right there. You see how smooth that was?

So, like everything in life, it all comes down to timing. Much later on you will realize that timing . . . and those tiny packs of raisins . . . are everything. You will depend on both and be unable to function without them. But when you start telling people, it *really* hits you. There is an approximate date set for your baby's birthday. Wait, should I start planning the first birthday now? Should I book that events company I heard about? I really need to call Elie Saab *now* and ask him how long he needs to custom-make her first tutu or his first tuxedo, right? Don't worry, I didn't. Okay, so I may have drafted an email that started with: "Dear Elie, I'm pregnant and your designs are amazing. Let's design a fall line together?" Cringe.

As it all sinks in, you go into staring into the future/tuning out mode. I would like to think of myself as a fun wife. Psychotic at times, yes, but generally fun. When we first got married I loved the group dinners. Retrospectively, they were fun but perhaps not the best use of my time as a newlywed—I could have been fluent in Czech by now or learnt how to ride a bike. Don't look so appalled, I ended up learning how to ride a bike, just late. Hey, since when is last month considered too late?

But, pregnant me? I'm tuning out of the group conversations and staring into space as I imagine pushing this baby out of my lady bits.

I never knew what it would feel like or how I would feel being kicked by that leg I was busy growing. How preoccupied and obsessed by it I would be, but it happened while friends were over for a regular wine and cheese night. Except I could no longer enjoy the wine or the cheese. Gnocchi kicked on Mother's Day. Wait, did this mean what I think it meant? That I'd be the best mama in the world? No, it meant that my baby was fluent in Morse code and was wishing me a happy Mother's Day. It also meant I was supposed to be sober at these get-togethers and have conversations with everyone. At least I could start pretending I'm not really lactose intolerant. God, that was tough. So, no, I wasn't exactly present at cheese nights anymore, but I got to enjoy forcing friends to hold their hands over my belly in case another kick happened.

How to Fake It at the Twelve-Week Scan

Twelve weeks have never been so important to me. It's a big scan and a lot happens in this timeframe between the five- to seven-week heartbeat scan to this momentous twelve-week bonanza of measurements taken, nuchal folds examined, and going from nothing to a freakish unquestionably human face. Here's where you see if baby's eyes and ears are in the right place and that they look a lot less like a Van Gogh painting. The baby in the making is just over two inches long, weighs half an ounce, and is the size of a lime. How appropriate since limes are still on my "can eat" list that has shrunk to four options. My whole life I've been bad at keeping secrets and now for the first time in my life I am kinda sorta okay keeping this one under the radar. So, I wait. I wait until the official go-ahead like the sign to take off from the airport traffic controller. The doctor checked and I was given the green light to spill the beans. Not so much with frantic oversized hand gestures, earmuffs, and those fluorescent yellow vests, but with a gentle half smile.

The twelve-week scan is like those Rorschach tests, where a psychologist shows you a collection of inkblots and what you see reveals your personality and emotional functioning. No pressure. I guess this would speak volumes about me because of how I "saw" Gnocchi on that scan. Dr. Annie pointed, saying, "There's your baby," to which I pointed to black nothingness and confidently said to my husband, "Oh my god, Gnocchi has your head shape, how cute!" This test plagued me for the months to come as I faithfully pretended every month to distinguish body parts because I didn't want my doctor and husband to think I was a bad mom. Yes, I faked it. Without fail, I shrieked and shouted, "Wowwww that's a leg . . . and the eyes . . . wait, you don't see it?" all while Mr. Excel struggled to get on the same page as me. My Rorschach results would be: *too competitive, needs Xanax.*

But this was such an easy test to cheat on. While my mouth was saying, "Gnocchi has your nose," my mind was thinking, *Ummm, is that a nose or foot? Why are there so many shadows?* I waited for cues from the doctor to which I would squeal, "Yeah, I see it!" and turn to Mr. Excel with disappointment that he couldn't see what I "saw." All in all, it was a lot of lying and awwwws and wows. I kept that up the entire pregnancy. No wonder I was so tired all the time.

Walking out of the twelve-week scan appointment I made a private pact to quit the "fake it till you make it" stuff (which I would later realize is such an integral Jenga piece to mommyhood) and admit that I was staring into a void here. Which only made me feel . . . unstable. Yes. It's hard to embrace that quality. *Hi there, I'm unstable!* Not cool. But I am. I'm irresponsible and never had a plant or fish survive longer than a week on my watch. Yet, here I was—carrying unborn life. A real human. A real person who would one day have an opinion about Pop-Tarts and macadamia nuts and poetry and car paint colors. I couldn't help but feel sorry for my unborn child.

Yes, I was fun, but I was *careless*. With a capital C. Oh, god, and I'm going to have to teach them why certain words start with C and others start with the letter K, but it's the same sound? Whaaaat? And with that would surely come a whole list of injuries. I wasn't so sure I would discourage her/him from jumping off the bed with a frying pan in one hand and a bucket of paint in the other. In fact, I could easily see myself cheering him or her on. JUMP! JUMP! JUMP! For both of our entertainment! Did that make me a bad mom before I was actually a mom? Or was I being realistic as to how many challenges I'd be facing . . . refraining from whooping as your kid jumps off the bed being a big one.

This is where your inner voice takes over your heart, mind, body, and any other part of you left to be ruled. These things are not in your hands. Self-doubt and the urgent need for reassurance become key to your survival and overall wellbeing. They were my newest real-life besties.

In flood the insecurities—again.

What if he or she's as bad at math as I am?
Will I ever get my body back?
What if I miss my old life?
What if she has my hair? Or he has my ears? (Oh, for the record, she does. And he does.)

Even these moments of extreme self-doubt have a magical feel to them. It. Is. Happening. And then like an elephant mama-in-training I am jolted back to a memory of a mom I saw one day: pregnant and crying at Eric Clapton. She was ingrained in my head. The age of her kids? One barely walking, one barely talking, and one barely registering on the ultrasound. I'm not sure what she was crying about, and I bet you she wasn't sure either. It might have been the weather, the music, or that she ordered a chocolate and banana crêpe and they left out the banana. Who knew.

When you see a mama like her, don't ask any questions, just give her a silent nod. It's motherhood code for "I wanna lose my shit here but I'm outnumbered by dependents—so I gotta suck it up and deal."

It was at this time that I also had my first elevator encounter in which a woman in my building asked me if I was pregnant and what I was having. I got so chatty and excited, speaking two hundred words a minute until we reached her floor that I was left in mid-sentence—hand on belly. Doors closed and I was still talking about the 4-D photos from my latest scan. I pulled it out and sent a voice note to my bestie in Mauritius about how Gnocchi looked to be doing some elaborate yoga pose. (Little did I know that this was foreshadowing of what was to come. Read more in Chapter 17.) In that moment, I remembered that it's our real-life besties who will really listen. And the overwhelm of emotions and being left mid-sentence will make you breakdown into a sob fest, but what else are you busy doing, anyway? It's okay. Rocking is optional.

So, there I was, staring at the numbers of the floors light up. Eight . . . fourteen . . . twenty-five . . . all the way from the tenth floor to the thirty-third I contemplated so much. What could I do to get more involved with UNICEF in the region? Why was TB still not eradicated? What was I going to order for dinner? Why did I have gas again? In that moment I knew what I had to do, so I did what many had done before me. I sent my bestie a pouty sad-face selfie. She replied with six sad-face emojis.

No, I wasn't a perpetually smiling, happy-go-lucky pregnant mom-to-be. Yes, my laughter did veer into ugly cries at times. No judging, remember? That pregnant glow women speak of was more the radiant warm flush of a sob fest in my case. Any moment I felt overwhelmed my tears welled, and then I would remind myself that crying is simply affordable makeup. It made my eyes a hazel green, cheeks pink, and lips red. I'll take it. And I continued to fake it.

The Power of Rubbing Your Belly

International families have international wedding destinations, dysfunctional conversations about tradition, and confusing beliefs about God, the afterlife, and what dishes raisins should be added into. We had a big family wedding coming up with Mr. Excel's brother marrying a Thai American woman. Their wedding date happened when I was fourteen weeks pregnant. And the destination? Thailand!

If I was having issues with smells in the office, Thailand was a whole other washing machine of parsley bits, weird-smelling fruit, and temple stairs. An olfactory nightmare. I was permanently dizzy and drenched in sweat. Oh, and having to pee endlessly. Needless to say, the bathrooms in Thailand are far from friendly. They were far and . . . well, far, and that was enough to make me hate them. I was the farthest thing from in my element and struggling to look cute in a flowy blue dress for the ceremony when it was so darn hot I could barely put any underwear on.

Meanwhile, Mr. Excel would have worn a similar flowy dress if his brother had let him—but this was his day. (His brother's—not Mr. Excel's.) Mr. Excel was already married. Ummm. To me. So, he had to wear tight-fitted traditional Thai formal wear for the ceremony to match what his brother wore. But, his brother got to ride in on an elephant. Guess who threw a tantrum here. It really was the perfect glimpse into those terrible twos. Except Mr. Excel was two plus thirty (and now a few more than that).

The hard part was everyone downing shots and being all happily intoxicated. I realized people are not as funny as I thought they were. Not being even the slightest bit un-sober is really sobering. On alcohol I love everyone. Like *love*. And high fiving is my chosen form of communication. Your name has an "A" in it, too? High five and SHAFADAAA (shot for that). In Thailand, I couldn't let FOMO (fear of missing out) take over so I persevered by doing water shots from weird-smelling glasses. There was a lot of high fiving awkwardness too. Why are high fives more coordinated when you are drunk?

We laughed a lot in Thailand, though, like laughed so much we cried . . . or was that sweat dripping into our eyes? I ended up rediscovering my roots in Thailand: old school hip-hop and a love of adventure. Things I probably shouldn't have done there include a scooter ride in Phuket, a creepy ping-pong show in Bangkok where there were more than a few women rubbing my belly saying "*giiiiiiiir insiiiii*" (girl inside) and climbing the steps of those temples in intense heat. I did the temple stairs mainly to prove a point I was still fit, and to laugh at how out of my breath Mr. Excel was each time. We bonded about being so out of breath. Me with a baby pressing on my bladder and him with last night's extra serving of pad thai pressing . . . no, rather, *adding* to his gut. Yep, by now you'll be noticing how much your partner's body is changing with this pregnancy, too. It becomes a battle of who is suffering more.

Forgetfulness, passing gas, burping, and being kicked in the bladder are all officially cute when you are pregnant. You can blame the baby for all of it. Other conditions are less charming, such as his man flu. Call it man flu, call it allergies, call it the ultimate testament to my nerves. Mr. Excel developed a cough—from Thailand onward. I called it a coping cough, like a whooping cough yet a lot more pathetic. He had it the entire six months until Gnocchi held his finger. It must have been a coping mechanism to deal with a "difficult situation"—a.k.a. becoming a daddy—but all I had to do was rub my belly to remind him who was the boss. Not him, not me, but this little lime.

How to Outlaw the In-Laws

Despite everything you can get away *with*, there is a certain category of people in your life that you cannot get away *from*, ever: enter the in-laws. I'm going to rip this page out of the copy I give them. Crap, this page and the whole of Chapter 8!

Your mom may not live near you. Even your in-laws may not live near you, but they *will* visit you. Breathe into it. Go to your happy place. Or pretend to be constipated and hide in your bathroom for hours at a time.

Ultimately, your mother-in-law's sole job, after continuing to raise your husband (whom, according to her cannot remember to eat three meals a day without direct supervision via FaceTime) is to tell you that everything you're doing is wrong. And she can see from the twelve-week scan that everything your unborn baby is doing will be *just* like your husband. "Ohmygod the way baby lifted its finger is exactly like Amore when he was a baby!"

They visit. They visit a lot. Like, really too much. And the worst part is that they have opinions. I mean, they *really* have opinions. And then these opinions make my husband and I fight. This is typically the way things go and, well, now that I am pregnant I have made a list of promises to myself that I really will try and keep. Well, most of them, anyway, but I swear if a woman tries to criticize my baby or tell me that I can't kiss them on the lips and talk to in a baby voice when he/she's thirty well, then, she's got to go.

Maybe we know the ways we *don't* want to be like our mother-in-law, but in what ways do we hope to emulate her? Figure out what her special gift is, her "currency." (Needlepoint cushions of kittens? Picking nettles out of the garden to make into soup? A love of margaritas?) Ply or douse her with her favorite thing (unless it's nettles) until she learns to love you one-tenth of the amount she loves her little boy. That's right, he's your grown husband, but still her little boy.

I thought it was an Arab thing that Arab moms obsess over their boys, but Indian mothers do it, Chinese and Jewish moms do it, as well as Catholic moms: the Italians, Greeks, and most of the Southern Hemisphere. What's the solution? You hope and pray you have a supportive husband. And don't hesitate to put him in check and deflate that ego like a too-old birthday balloon. You swear to yourself that when you are the MIL you won't be too bitchy to your sons' beloveds. Who am I kidding? I almost pushed a little girl at nursery today who was holding my second puzzle piece's hand (yes, he's a boy) while walking around the garden. I mean, you're fourteen months old already, Lara. Figure out how to walk on your own! Seriously.

So, the only way around a MIL is to project forward to the day you will be a MIL. I say save it all up—all of the opinions and interference and unsolicited advice. Karma is a bitch and dishing it back to the universe isn't so bad, is it? Let her ask where he ejaculated and speculate as to why it took so long to fall pregnant as much as she likes. I will be paying that forward in 2030.

HOW BADLY YOU WANT THIS

BADLY —

A BIT —

KINDA — WORLD PEACE

THAT ENTIRE PLATE OF CHEESE FRIES

YOUR EX TO SEE YOU LOOKING GORGEOUS AND ON A GOOD HAIR DAY

THE FRYMESTER

(SECOND TRIMESTER)

The second frymester is where you're kinda feeling a bit better about being pregnant. Congratulations, you can almost tolerate being around your husband. Your nausea has somewhat subsided and you're ready to ingest some food. Okay, at least more than a cracker or two. You're suddenly starving. As if you've never eaten before. You crave anything and everything fried. Deep fried. Double fried. Fried in butter batter and topped with fried salt. It is starting to get better for you at this point and now you actually understand why people have more than one child. I mean, at least a little bit more than during those moments of dry heaving over a toilet. Or trash can. Or your friend's purse.

7

HOW MANY WALNUTS DiD EiNSTEiN'S MAMA EAT?

(MONOPOLY MAMA)

So much of pregnancy is based on unicorn-infested theories and rainbow equations. My advice is to take them all with a grain of pink Himalayan salt. Welcome to your second trimester. This is the honeymoon phase of pregnancy because you look and feel your best. You're not so much thinking about how to keep stuff down as about what to send your husband out for. Go ahead and have a few plates of fries, but be sure and give that bump some goodness, too. And, no, ketchup doesn't count as a vegetable even if there's a picture of a tomato on the bottle.

I have to say, I have one of the most thoughtful husbands ever. No typos here. This morning I woke up with the usual difficulty. It was the kind of morning that starts with fifteen snooze alarms going off simultaneously. This was followed by a bout of depression and self-loathing after going through my closet of bland, conservative work clothes. A perk of working for the UAE Government. I spent a few minutes gazing at some short colorful dresses with the passing thought that I would not be able to fit into them much longer. A tight D&G dress to the movies? Why not!

Before I could rush out to work I was stopped by Mr. Excel who handed me a paper bag: Gnocchi's lunch.

Well, I found it cute for all of twenty seconds until I realized what he packed inside was all "nutritional value" stuff taken verbatim from my "puke list." Where was the peanut butter? The honeyroasted cashews? Instead he put in walnuts and some cheese slices. For Gnocchi's brain development. Let me back up a minute to explain my lifelong relationship to things of "nutritional value." Don't get me wrong, I'm all about being healthy. I just hate people telling me what to do—and eating falls under that.

I think a part of why I hate being bossed around is because I'm the youngest in my family of three kids. My big brother and sister are seven and five years older than me, respectively. And yes, I used to copy them and follow them around, which of course bothered them. I'm sure it still bothers them. It actually still bothers *me* and I blame my cuticle-biting habit on my sister to this day. Even before getting pregnant my sister's recurring line to me was that I needed to kick my ramen-noodles-for-dinner habit and "consume meals of nutritional value." I'm sure she wasn't talking about cuticle skin. (I know. Gross. Sorry.) But I'm also a big believer that nutrition is also consumed by the mind and heart through our thoughts. Capisce? And so, I decided that with every spoonful of Haagen-Dazs ice cream, I would think a positive thought, and laugh hysterically. It all counts toward developing a healthy fetus, right? You learn to ignore the stares.

My sister and my brother gave me the typical "little sister complex." One of my strongest childhood memories was them telling me I wasn't allowed to *touch* the Monopoly board, or the police would come take me away because it was for ages seven and up. I was six and a half. Then, they would try and convince me to touch it while forcing me to eat lamb's brain (a dish my mom used to have to bribe us to eat, understandably). Here's where I have to say a huge thank-you to American anti-Monopolist Elizabeth Magie for creating the rage-encouraging game in 1903 and another huge thank-you to the inventor of Tang for giving me something to wash the one bite of lamb's brain down with.

So, here I was, second trimester, getting major flashback of Monopoly games gone wrong and trying to call one of my siblings to bitch about them it. I was finally getting some attention (mostly medical) from my big brother because I now had something meaningful—pregnancy—to talk to him about (other than the times I was hungover and convinced I was having a stroke) because he is a doctor. I think he saw me as the perpetual immature baby of the family, even though the first time I lived alone was when I was fifteen. Yes. It was in a strict all-girls catholic boarding school, which gave me the perfect chance to learn how to break rules, keep calm, and work on my synchronized menstruation skills.

I didn't know at the time and barely knew later, to be honest. But what *did* I know? "Being a mother is the hardest job on earth. Women everywhere must declare it so." I only knew that because I read Oprah's book, *What I Know for Sure*. Preach on Oprah, preach on. I wonder what wise words she would have to say about order of birth or sibling rivalry. What would be her take on Monopoly, oral fixations, and the fact that I contact my brother and sister (in some form or another) every day? Should we encourage her to address all that in her next book?

It's Not You, It's Me . . . Breaking Up with WebMD

One of the biggest milestones of any mommy-to-be's journey is (cue dramatic music) the sex reveal party. Nobody really cares you are pregnant, but everyone wants to know if their guess on gender is correct.

Speculation goes like this:

"What do you eat and crave? Dairy? Ahhhh, then it's a girl."

"All you wanted to eat were sour things and you couldn't stand your husband? You're going to have a boy!"

"Tie a hair to your wedding ring and hold it over the belly. If it goes in circles it's a girl, if it sways back and forth it's a boy." Or is it the other way around? Any swaying movement at all is confirmation you're at least pregnant.

"Ass the size of a planet? Girl."

"Belly button has disappeared completely? Boy."

"Plagued by zits and cat dreams? Girl."

I got numerous, "Ohhh wow . . . you look . . . amazing . . . for sure it's a girl . . . you look . . . completely different. I almost didn't recognize you." Um, thanks? Is that code for "Holy crap you look like a hot mess, that better be a girl inside!"

There are countless traditions and tests online that one can undergo to find out the sex of a baby, but I didn't believe I'd need any of them. I believed all those women in Thailand rubbing my belly with their creepy *"giiiiiiiir insiiiii"* echoing in my thoughts. I'm not sure if these other online tests are found on WebMD, probably not, actually, but who else am I going to blame for medical misinformation? Yes, I'm pulling the "it was on the Internet so has to be true" card.

This is the moment in this chapter where I make you take a quiz. Don't skim it. Studies have shown that the findings of these quizzes have been proven to cause smiles and smirks.

Here's how you can predict the gender of your baby. One-hundred percent correct every time:

1) When you look in your closet you see it's predominantly:
   a) black and studded items with a whole lot of leather
   b) ruffles, lace, and anything in pastel colors

2) When imagining a family vacation, you envision:
   a) a combination of hiking, fishing, and camping. You are okay with the prospect of cold coffee and scraped knees
   b) anywhere you can wear all of your 432 frilly dresses

3) Bedtime story time with your nieces or nephews is a chance to:
   a) do backward somersaults and make loud firetruck noises and monster faces
   b) get snuggly and talk about bunny kisses.

Mostly As: you are having a girl.
Mostly Bs: you are having a boy.

I really wanted to leave the gender reveal as a surprise until Gnocchi's birth, but I wasn't allowed. I negotiated hard, but Mr. Excel prevailed. I kinda saw his point, but part of the beauty of your first pregnancy is the novelty of it and also having the time to daydream. Often imagining what sort of baby girl or boy's mama you will be.

Our appointment finally arrived for the gender reveal scan and I hear myself reminding my MIL (and every Arab female relative in my family) that girl or boy it's a win-win situation. When I lead by example with, "I would be happy with either," my MIL responds, "No, no, me too, but more happy with a boy. Like much more. Really I will be heartbroken if it's a girl." I didn't want to tell her that I was convinced Gnocchi was a girl.

The waiting room was packed with several couples like us filling out a form and waiting. I am always amazed at the instant bonding this provokes. Okay, I know that's not saying much coming from me because I am known to become best friends with anyone in the span of five seconds. I go wash my hands/pee and come back ten minutes later with a new girlfriend's number, her whole life story, and lunch plans for next Saturday. We flush and exchange pet peeves and stories about what makes us tick. We divulge our innermost secrets. A tight hug and we go our separate ways. And by separate ways I mean everlasting friendship nourished by WhatsApps and long voice notes.

I do love those waiting room questionnaires though because I always want to fill in the right answer. Don't forget, I'm competitive and always wanna win. I'm in it to win it, yes. The top question after name and nationality is usually "how you got pregnant" and I always look for a box to tick marked "it was dark and I was drunk" or "we had five minutes before my MIL's latest visit began" but nothing. All that I see is a column of expensive-sounding scientific conception assistance and clinical grade-school terminology. How disappointing. Someone needs to rewrite these forms and language to help pregnant women laugh through it all, don't you think? It's like they *want* to make it sound intimidating to keep us—barefoot and pregnant?

Then you go in and your 56,453 mommy-worry thoughts are quieted by one word that baby's measurements are "Normal."

And we look. And Gnocchi is a girl.

It is incredible to find out the sex and return to the same waiting room and essentially share this news with complete strangers first before your own family.

Oh, but to compensate for the lack of being a boy, my MIL wants me to name her Rania. *Her* name is Rania. Need I say more? I'm just not sure what she wants the shrine to be made of. Did I not take enough *za'atar* before this test?

For those of you who don't know, *za'atar* (thyme) is also something all Arabs agree on. The long-standing tradition is to eat *za'atar* before a test and never before a dentist appointment. So yes, eating it by the spoonful, spread on a sandwich, or sprinkled in our coffee (not so much) became integral to passing any exam. I guess that tradition somehow also made its way to major doctor's appointments. Basically, anytime you need to get good results and are in need of a boost in brain function, you must make use of that toothpick and befriend that herb.

And then the prayers began. Mostly in the form of things I hoped she *didn't* have. We debated it. I hoped she had anyone's nose but mine. And that she didn't have my Dumbo ears that I had surgically (unsuccessfully, I might add) pinned back when I was fifteen. As if I wasn't insecure enough, the "Inshallahs" started rolling in as soon as people found out that I was having a girl. So many Inshallahs that I couldn't begin or end a sentence without it. Inshallah is used for any future event and this was a future event so why not go ahead and paint my pregnancy with it. All it means is "God willing" and so yes, God willing she would have my fast metabolism and not my weird elbows or dislike of dill, among other things. And God willing I would have a boy after this trial go at baby-making. (I did—I had two.) And the Inshallahs naturally evolved to where they're at now—praying that I will have a fourth child. Another girl. It. Is. Never. Ending.

Maybe this is the universe's cruel way to get you to love everything about yourself—it chooses the one quality or body part you hate about yourself and reproduces it. Suddenly you have to pivot on your stance on big Dumbo ears and come to see them as cute and charming when accompanied with an oversized pink flower headband. You research and quickly find big ears are a sign of intelligence in some countries (okay, it's in Burkina Faso).

I was really happy to be having a girl. I was just nervous. Would she want to be like me or the complete opposite of me? Today's world is hard—would she have the backbone and hunger to want to try to do it all? In those 4-D scans you can see your little one smile and yawn and move around. Typically, the movements the baby does in the womb are pretty much what they do when they're born. No smiles or yawns with our Gnocchi, though, instead she whipped up a series of ballet positions. As a former ballerina (okay, not a serious one, but I owned several tutus) I was excited. Maybe we would be the first mother-daughter duet to make it to the New York Ballet! Yes, my imagination took me that far.

Don't You Know You're Toxo-Immune?

Britney Spears really knew what she was talking about. "I'm addicted to you don't you know that you're toxic? It's getting late to give to you up I took a sip from my devil's cup." I mean, you'd have to be crazy not to think she was talking about wine and cheese, right?

So, apart from those big important scans you go through when you're pregnant—there are the constant blood tests . . . a biggie is the test for toxoplasmosis. When my results came back negative I high-fived Mr. Excel and immediately called my sister to gloat that I aced the test.

"It came back negative. I don't have it."

She came back with, "No, dummy, that means you haven't come in contact with the virus and are susceptible to getting it DO NOT POKE YOUR BROTHER WITH THAT FORK. AND PULL YOUR PANTS BACK UP!"

[Click]

Ah, the pros and cons of being non-toxo-immune. Ordering in a restaurant would take me so long I was ready to eat a horse *tartare*. "What's in this? Oh, the fennel gratin includes uncooked shaved fennel in it? Um . . . yeah, no, I can't have that." (Insert sheepish smile.) "Yeah I can't have anything uncooked because of the risk of toxoplasmosis." (Insert fifteen-minute explanation of what it is). By this time, you're ready to eat the waiter's arm. (Well-done, not raw.)

Toxo this, toxo that. I'm over it. There is an element of coolness that pregnancy comes with and some of that coolness is taken away when you run the risk of contracting a horrible illness like toxo. Or is it? You're kinda more in the limelight because you have to talk to the waiter for forty-five minutes about what you can and cannot eat. Thrilling. Bring it on, you're making a life. You. No one else, just you. Something is growing inside of you. Why shouldn't you be the center of attention?

Yeah, but no.

The edicts about what you can and cannot eat in pregnancy is every woman's chance to be (wait for it and cue the marching band parade) dramatic focused on self-care. According to my MIL and grandmother it is all nonsense. The total abstention from alcohol and avoiding cat feces. Regardless, at any restaurant where the raw parsley touched the grilled fish, my "Send it back" felt like I was being a bit of a drama queen and waiting for a bunch of Oompa Loompas to roll up singing, "Save the baby and send it backkkkkkkk . . . order something well cooked . . . like lamb of rackkkkkk!"

I will, however, stick to my stance of strongly believing women should not be treated like three-year-olds, airily instructed in the way of things with no proper evidence-based statistical explanation, whether pregnant or not. After all, stress is actually worse for a fetus than a glass of wine, according to an article I read in . . . okay, my mama told me. I also heard that this is a good reason to run away to a yoga retreat, although that is definitely not advice to follow. At least not before the baby is born.

That's why I drank the occasional espresso. And by occasional, I mean often. Like twice a day. Imminent motherhood changes our perspectives on life, we all know this. But, it's true. The things that used to stress me out no longer do. Okay, that's a lie. I still stress, but I get over the triggers much quicker. Like seven days quicker and after only three outbursts. That's improvement. It's okay to take an hour to order. It's okay to overreact and then forget why you're mad and tell the waiter you're *allergic* to parsley. Tomato, Tomato. You know, like the song? "You say tomato . . . I say tomato." Yeah, you get it.

8
MY MANTRA FOR DEALING WITH MY MIL

Ugh.

9

CAN'T TOUCH THIS, UNLESS YOU ARE MC HAMMER

(DENIAL, CAN WE BREAK UP YET?)

Sometime around month five, the touching begins. I don't know you and neither does my baby—please don't touch. Like, seriously, get your hand off. But, if you respect my wishes and don't touch I will become paranoid and wonder whyyyyy you didn't extend your sometimes manicured otherwise typically gummy hand to touch my blessed bump? Do I not constitute a cute-enough pregnant woman for you? And enter parenting paranoia. A phenomenon that takes days and even months to dissolve.

There are so many opinions about strangers touching belly bumps. Most people are kind and polite enough to ask first. I however often felt offended if people *didn't* want to touch my belly. Mr. Excel was afraid I would start screaming, "TOUCH ITTTTT" at random strangers. A good rule of thumb is to ask first. Especially in situations where the pregnant woman is shoving her round navel in your face. Asking convinces her she was actually discreet.

The one exception to this rule is when it's other pregnant women reaching out to touch. There is an unspoken camaraderie between all pregnant women. There's that knowing look and smile we give each other as we pass by, so I say if another pregnant woman wants to touch the belly she can go right ahead, but that door is only open to those of us in the knocked-up club.

We'll be talking more about touching and universal truths a little later, but I will say that, on this chaotic and barely manageable journey, you will throw more than a few universal truths out the window. And *that* is a universal truth if not *the* universal truth. Just go ahead and throw it out the window. It's okay. I know I am one ball of mixed metaphors. How about this one: Get in the flow and stay in it.

So, it's month five and you've been trying to keep it real but also not overdo it. God, that line is so hard. I've been trying to revert to being a normal person now that most of my puking is over. Most of it. Don't high five me yet. I want to enjoy "stuff," as in, life in general, before turning into a "whale" like everyone says. Why a whale, people, why? Why can't the comparison be to an attractive and overly ambitious sleek bird or a cute lemur? But, no . . . we're always compared to that whale. I get it. It's the weight gain. But how unoriginal is that? And really, the last thing I feel like doing is swimming mostly because of the struggle of putting your bathing suit on and then peeling it off to pee once it's wet. Don't pretend for a second that you haven't stood in a shower stall and contemplated sleeping in your bathing suit to skip having to peel off that synthetic extra "skin." I've been stuck there with it around my thighs often and have to take a break and hang out in my bathroom halfway through the process. Not my proudest or sexiest moment, no. Let's just say it . . . my attempt at prenatal yoga has been just that. Attempts and a bit of denial because I refuse to give in and admit that I can't do certain things because I am "with child" and uncoordinated, like I said. Denial is really sad. A pregnant woman in denial about what she can and cannot do is really, *really* sad. That's two reallys, guys. No typos. At least I had the weight gain under control, except my MIL voiced fears of Gnocchi coming out with malnutrition because I wasn't eating bread and butter with rice and noodles topped in maple syrup sauce. That's apparently all she ate when she was pregnant with my husband. Could that maybe be the reason why he loves IHOP? You just can't win.

I was also in denial about buying maternity clothes. I would get dressed for a casual jeans and tennis shoes type of dinner an hour before we would have to leave because I knew that zipping up those skinny jeans would take time. And patience. But mostly me lying down on my bed in all sorts of weird squat positions wriggling around aggressively in never-before-seen angles. You go out and buy something, except two sizes bigger, and because you're intending this to be temporary, as cheap as possible. You will find two outfits and repeat wear them until they disintegrate. Thank you, Denial! Can we break up yet?

Buying maternity clothes . . . as in, stocking up on comfy hoodies and cute lounge pants came in handy, given the temperature of my bedroom. Up until this point, my whole marriage was a game of temperature tug-of-war. My pj's closely resemble a thermal ski suit: socks and hoodie included. Don't get me wrong, I might have sexy lingerie on—depending—underneath, but this was only revealed for all of five minutes before reaching for my North Face ski mask. My husband loves air-conditioning and refuses to sleep without it, a side effect of spending his schooldays at the American School in Saudi Arabia. Now, I love me some AC, but prefer it at a normal temperature: what I imagine a cool breeze off the Amalfi coastline to feel like. You know, a breeze generated by attractive men casually strolling past me on the white sandy beach with their oiled-up six packs and perfect tans . . . pressing a fresh piña colada into my hand. Wait, what was my point here? Oh, yes, so I milked the AC war. I was not going to be the first pregnant woman to wear a ski suit to bed. The temperature heated up a whole five degrees in our bedroom. And that's no innuendo.

Pilates My Ass

Then, I started Pilates with a private instructor. I wish you could see me rolling my eyes in retrospect. Close your eyes and imagine it. Yes, I have big brown eyes and my lashes are usually covered in mascara. (It just makes me feel better, okay?) So, the Pilates. It's been annoying. No, unbelievably annoying. I don't give a poop about my spine, I would just like you to perform some sort of magic trick to make me less inflexible, uncoordinated, and an absolute klutz. I'm usually okay with these qualities and I'd like to think that this has somehow translated into a bit of charm. Do not ask me how I managed to be the star of my ballet recital and wow everyone with my interpretation of *Little Red Riding Hood*. I did. They were wowed. It was a moment. I still relive it and tell it at dinner parties. The best part is that the costume still fits (not really because I was eleven).

Mr. Excel does not let me bring that out to dinner parties. Unless I'm already wearing it. I wanted a photo of me in it as the cover of this book, but my publishers shot that down. Something about frizz and always blinking right at the very moment the camera snapped the picture. What do people call that again? Oh, unphotogenic. You know, someone who looks totally different in a photo than they do in real life. *Unphoto*: hating photos and *genic:* generally, looks like crap in them at any and every occasion, especially birthdays, weddings, anniversaries, and anything they're tagged in on social media.

So yes, staying fit during my three back-to-back pregnancies has been a priority for me, but mainly because I heard what three back-to-back pregnancies does to your bones, hair, teeth, and nails. Thanks to a combination of FlyBarre classes, Physique 57, Barry's Bootcamp, a Pilates instructor, and a live-in trainer, I have been doing okay. (They better all agree to selling my book in their studios after this plug.) I know you're probably thinking: Who can afford or has the time for all of that? The truth is that I don't, but if I don't make it a priority to exercise I will murder someone and the lawyering up will be a far bigger cost than paying for these memberships. I often cancel one or all of those appointments during the week, but the intention is there. I feel fitter just seeing the reminder for the appointment, but I'm thankful there's no app where messages pop up saying, "Hey, what's going on . . . you're missing another class?" Thank God there isn't, although I'm sure someone's bitter ex-boyfriend in Nebraska is figuring out the algorithm for it right this second.

But, staying active, yes. It's for my own amusement also. I've been scaring my husband into getting a bit healthier and have created some worthy shortcuts to get Mr. Excel to the gym. And yes, to do something other than chitchat there. I've got a friend who hates working out with her husband because he drips sweat onto everything and barely talks while doing a dead lift. I'm convincing myself that's not why Mr. Excel goes to the gym. But then, thinking about it, it's a definite potential break for him from my chattiness. No wonder he is currently training for a marathon.

So, on the occasion that I was trying to be all nice, I offered Mr. Excel my fly wheel sessions and his response was, "Wait, you're gonna need them afterward." He probably will too at the rate his weight gain is going. Is that called *preggo by proxy* or just sheer laziness? Alas, despite all the working out that was supposed to increase endorphins and seratonins and oxytoxins and chilledoxins and don'tloseyourshitins, it officially happened.

I had my big psycho pregnancy moment.

It's funny how you never think you'll be that girl—but somehow or other there is a shift in your sanity (a.k.a. hormones, and you morph into that girl). BLAME IT ON THE HORMONES always. Pre-pregnancy, during pregnancy, post-pregnancy, and post-post-pregnancy. Hormones are the reason for everything from now on. Forever.

Every mama, or 99 percent of them, has this one big psycho pregnancy moment. It's okay.

I'm talking about the big moment they will live down until the day they die. Mine came when Mr. Excel ate the last marshmallow chocolate chip cookie. Hang on. Give me a moment. Let me breathe through this one. Let's just say that he was mid-chew when I mounted his back, hyena style. He laughed so much he choked—and then accused me of blocking off his airway.

Here's some critical math for you . . . or mathematical magic as I like to call it. Wait, are you cringing? Do I sound like your great aunt at Thanksgiving who's showing you how to remove a stain and wants it to sound cooler than it is so she calls it magic? Go ahead and write down your answers for this one anyway, even if you are cringing. Truthfully. I'll tell you what it indicates afterward.

Count the number of pregnancy tests you have done: 13

Now, multiply it by the number of times you have contemplated killing your partner today: $13 \times 14 = 182$

Now, take that number and add the number of times you have peed today: $182 + 15 = 197$

Number of calls you have ignored from your mother-in-law: 14

Add it to the number of calls you have ignored from your sister in law: 8

Now, add it to your other number: $14 + 8 + 197 = 219$

Add it to the number of plans made and canceled today: $219 + 8 = 227$

Multiply it by number of times you've touched your belly today: $227 \times 525 = 119,175$

Congratulations! Any score above 28 means you are officially ready to have your big psycho pregnancy moment (or half day, really). You are in the land of cray cray. Nooo, in the cutest way. The pregnancy land of cray cray is a safe place. With nice houses and an unlimited supply of chocolate. At least, there *better* be the chocolate or that will trigger your big psycho pregnancy moment. Let's just call it your BPPM. That's in WebMD, pinkie promise.

Navel Gazing

Everyone who's about to step into a room full of people they don't know asks themselves if they're going to be liked. Wait, is that just me? When pregnant you analyze who you are in terms of what kind of mama you'll be. Like, 23,649 times per day. It's a lot of getting out that mirror and looking inside. No, not like those mamas in the seventies checking out their vaginas in the mirror. My ob-gyn told me to write down the type of child we wanted to have. This confused me. Wanted to have? Like I could choose? She was just warming us up though because next came the more useful exercise where you write down the five things you want to repeat about how your parents were with you, and five things you do not, like, everrrrr want to repeat. I had to sit down for this. I was already sitting, but you get what I mean. This was like therapy. I kinda loved it.

Here are how my lists looked:

What I want to repeat:

1. I learned how to swim when my daddy threw me in the pool and shouted, "*YALLA* SWIM MOVE YOUR ARMS AND LEGS." Sometimes old-school is the best school. Safety is not always first.
2. Having my back and always making me feel covered—even if they fought and yelled with insurance for not covering my latest car accident. (Sidenote: Get insured.)
3. I grew up believing problems were nothing more than real-life puzzles. As in, everything has a solution—you just have to put the pieces alongside each other or together in a different way to solve the whole picture.

4. Eating time is a time to chew but also talk. To talk about everything from what we learned that day to the importance of grape leaves in our diet.
5. Socks are reversible for a reason.

What I do *not* want to repeat:

1. Instill false confidence in them. I really thought I had a phenomenal singing voice until last year. I just don't know when I got so tone-deaf. Wait, did I *not* wow the crowd as Little Red Riding Hood?
2. Make them feel entitled. Like life owes them something. Except, damn it, they will have a harsh wake-up call soon enough. Say things like, "You get five sips of water and three toilet paper squares today. You're welcome."
3. Doubt their capabilities. So what if they don't put on their own shoes until they're seventeen? They'll get married soon enough and it'll be someone else's problem.
4. Pretending that wasabi is avocado to make them eat a big blob.
5. Give you a haircut without asking. I mean, why would a nine-month-old need bangs?

Sorry, that was a lot of me-me-me. And a lot about my Daddy. I promise he is the coolest person you'd ever meet . . . and probably the most *not* PC. And, anyway, pregnancy *is* the perfect time to be a little narcissistic and gain perspective on your own family experiences—mostly because no one will call you out on it.

10

HOW MUCH WILL SHE HATE US iF WE NAME HER HASHTAG?

(WHERE'S THE PARTY AT? GOODNiGHT!)

Sit down, breathe deep, and go ahead and look smug. You've survived the first half of pregnancy. Go ahead and pat yourself on the back. Oh, you can't reach . . . umm okay, relax . . . don't get annoyed. Just smile and bask in: "you done good gurl."

It's human nature to feel a sense of relief when you reach the halfway point in something. You hit mile twenty-one of a marathon and all of a sudden, you're like, I've got this. I've trained so hard. It's mind over matter. It's now or never. The competition is with the weak. Or, maybe there's a voice in your head telling you to stop. I have yet to run a complete marathon, but I can say that the same feeling rushes over me when I'm halfway through a sandwich or an episode of *Game of Thrones*. I'm warmed up. I'm like, hell yeah, I can finish the other half of this panini. It's all about continuity anyway, you're in it now so you may as well finish. However, when I reached the halfway point in my pregnancy, though, I have to say . . . I did not have that same rush.

Halfway point? Um, wait, you mean I still have twenty weeks to go? I'm already over it. Sorry, Gnocchi, but I miss sushi. Yes, sushi. Sushi and skydiving, actually. Okay, so skydiving I don't really miss because I only did it once (thirtieth birthday surprise) but, still, just having the option to do it again . . . like tomorrow would be nice.

Come to think of it, you're halfway through this book. Unless you're cheating and skipping around? That's completely allowed, by the way, no rules with me. Didn't I tell you I'm not going to mention rules? Ummm none, other than please read all of this book, write to me, let me know what you loved (or hated), and spread the love. And by spread the love I mean email everyone on your contact list and tell them to buy it, read it, and write me a phenomenal review. Too much? My therapist and everyone in my life seems to think I have a problem understanding the concept of less is more. I bought fourteen books to read up on this issue in the hopes of finding an answer that will resonate with me. I'm still on page sixteen of the first book, but hopeful.

Wait, does anyone even read anymore? Something tells me that we're all so busy scrolling and swiping, double tapping, and commenting with lame emojis that we're not using our brains anymore. Don't get me wrong, I think social media is great. I mean, most of the time. And for certain things, sure. But the rest of the time? Well, I think we need to look around, look up, and possibly, just possibly use our hands for something else. You know, to hold something other than our phones maybe? Just maybe.

Social media, you've kept me up like a newborn. You've made me feel insecure with your fake rainbows and unicorn compositions. And what's with your myriad of tiled floors with cute pointy shoes? Oh, and don't get me started with your little babies and perfect bodies. With your filters and enhancers and advertising campaigns. It's been seriously exhausting. On most days I can't bear to hear people ask if they know you. Or rather if they #knowyou.

Dear lifestyle blogger, I love your hair and smile but I'm exhausted just looking at your pictures. Perfection, yes, but you're setting such a high standard that I have to put my phone down and remind myself that I'm happy with my neither straight nor wavy locks (if I can even call them locks—it's more like my three remaining strands of hair after three back-to-back pregnancies and having kids who force me to hide in my bathroom to eat chocolate and run the tap so it sounds like I'm doing something else). You make me malcontent with my coffee-stained jeans and sloppy, frazzled mom look that really ought to be a trend—any day now.

Dear five million hits for cats. Listen, I'm trying to do something here. I'm trying to find my tribe, but my tribe are busy chuckling over how cute you furry ones are. So what if you meow so you look like you're talking? We get it. Many kittens before you and many after you will be doing the same thing. How can I compete with you when you leap into the air at the sight of a cucumber? What even is that?

Dear new thought guru, yes, I agree we all need that rainbow of love you've articulated but why can't you spell properly? Why substitute real words with those emojis? What does that little alien face even mean? You is spelled y-o-u, not u. Get help, and a dictionary.

Rant over. Sorta. Sorry, just had to get that off my chest. Really hope you're not going to unfollow me for that. I just . . . well, had to put that out there. Just to let you know that sometimes it's a little too much. A little too fast. A little too fake. And that (don't hate me for what I'm going to say next) being famous on Instagram is like being rich in Monopoly.

So, think of this book as a break! I promise you can go back to scrolling when it's done. And then you can comment on my page or blog or post something about how people need to buy this book. #TheNextAustinKleon.

Why is it that everyone else's pregnancy experiences on social media seem bigger, faster, stronger . . . dare I say better? I am not a jealous person by nature, but I am someone who is used to bench-marking. I can't help but feel that other people's pregnancies go at the speed of light: one minute you hear about it and think, "Wow that was fast/slow/about average" or "She's so old/young/about right" and *wham* the next second you have endless photos on Facebook led by the key central photo of a blissed out/drugged person in back-less hospital wear holding a baby that is beetroot red and covered in white gunk that looks like papier-mâché, with a whole head of hair (that notion of post-birth baby still grosses me out). Before you know it, you're flooded with about a million minute-by-minute tweets, hashtags, and perfectly curated posts. What is with that word anyway? *Curated*. Are we museum directors?

I'm sure many actually enlist a social media team for their preg-nancy and birth. You must've seen the job postings on www.dubi-zzle.com: Urgently needed: Social media manager for a minimum duration of nine months with possibility to extend for life. Good pay and possible bump touching included. Must be ready to Photoshop the sh*t out of every stretch mark and blemish.

Truth is, I need to filter my husband at this stage. What I used to find charming I now find absolutely annoying, like his blank stare. I can't even tolerate it. My list of things that have transitioned from charming and kinda fun to annoying to Oh-God-please-stop-doing-right-now-before-I-lose-it is getting longer. Among my top five this week are: Mr. Excel. All of him. For no reason. My cousin Jassem and how he tries to lift me every time he sees me. I love you but please stop. The coffee barista. The doorman from Uganda who I used to talk about gorilla sightings with. The doorman from Kenya who thinks asking me if I know what *caribou* means every day is charming or funny or both. It's neither. I now find it all annoying. All of it. Every last encounter.

When You Decide to Give Birth in Another Country

So, after hours and hours of discussions with all 731 of my relatives, I decided to deliver Gnocchi in Beirut. Not in Dubai where we live. Yes, 2,000 miles from home. With all of the inconvenience that would mean, all 731 of my relatives were like, of course. All 1,863 of his were less than thrilled. Okay, if you gasped and are thinking *Whyyy?* you are clearly not Middle Eastern. If you skimmed over that line casually thinking *mmhmm*, and then, *who was your doctor?*, you are clearly Lebanese or at least part. My mom is Lebanese and because she is based there as is my sister I chose to deliver there. Ummm, let me rephrase that, I fought with my husband for months prior to my due date about delivering there. Let me just get preachy for a moment here and tell you ladies to stand your ground because I personally did not want anyone in the delivery other than my mom and sister in that particular moment. Mr. Excel was there, of course, but within a matter of seconds I learned that there was really no need for his pale complexion and wide-eyed worry stare. Endearing, yes, but completely unnecessary.

It's a very Lebanese thing to not let yourself go to hell and deteriorate when you are giving birth. We call it continuing to take care of yourself through pregnancy and childbirth and well after. It's really the anti–Jenny McCarthy way—if that even was a way— of girls don't poop and if we do it smells nice and is not trauma- tizing or embarrassing in any way. Don't criticize or judge me here because it's just the way. You know what I'm talking about, right? *That* kind of sugarcoating. I actually got my nails and hair done the day after I delivered. Yeah, I know . . . I had to wait a day. Shocking, right? I mean, my hair was blow dried but restyled for the first-day photos, but at least my French manicure stayed fresh until I was discharged.

Sure, it's different priorities, but I also believe in the notion that you need to dress the part that you want and look how you want to feel. My second was an emergency C-section so I was already all dolled up and ready for the impromptu "first photoshoot with baby" because I was barely checked in and he was out in forty-five minutes. He has glitter on his face in some of the earlier pictures but I swear we looked good with my sparkly eye shadow and his faux hawk. Considerate boy for deciding to make an appearance when we were on our way to dinner. By my third birth I had the system down with both eyes all mascaraed up. And why wouldn't I have a bit of blue eyeliner on to match my hospital gown? You rolling your eyes yet?

Wait, we're still friends, right?

Things were approaching "real" but knowing I'd be giving birth in another country did keep it kinda magical and faraway sounding. I didn't know what to expect but I knew that I'd have my mom to cry to, my sister to vent to, my brother to tell me lovingly to suck it up and be unemotional about it, and my dad to keep me grounded with his occasionally lame and always repetitive jokes.

Questions to Ask Yourself When Deciding Where to Give Birth

At the end of the day *you* have to decide. It's one of the many decisions you're going to have to make for the benefit of your child without them being very involved. Naming them is another one, along with their first haircut. You can deny your involvement in these decisions later and swear on . . . well, their life that you had nothing to do with it. They won't believe you. Does therapy have a minimum age?

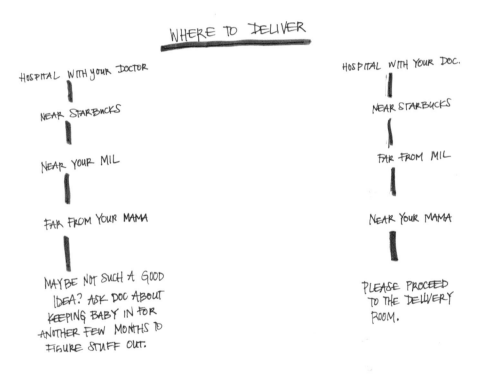

WHERE TO DELIVER

HOSPITAL WITH YOUR DOCTOR

NEAR STARBUCKS

NEAR YOUR MIL

FAR FROM YOUR MAMA

MAYBE NOT SUCH A GOOD IDEA? ASK DOC ABOUT KEEPING BABY IN FOR ANOTHER FEW MONTHS TO FIGURE STUFF OUT.

HOSPITAL WITH YOUR DOC.

NEAR STARBUCKS

FAR FROM MIL

NEAR YOUR MAMA

PLEASE PROCEED TO THE DELIVERY ROOM.

NEEDS VS. WANTS

NEED

WANT

BREAST PUMP
COT

SPA SESSIONS

BRACELETS

THE BUYMESTER
(THIRD TRIMESTER)

The third buymester is when panic mode sets in. You have been so worried about all the tests until now that not only have you essentially not enjoyed the entire journey, but you have also not bought anything on all the lists you researched and printed out from the thousands of "useful links" you've bookmarked. Suddenly you are Russell Crowe from that scene in *A Beautiful Mind*. You rattle off numbers and objects and where to find them all with messy arrows mapping out your "efficient trip to the mall" where you convince your husband you can purchase and finish everything in an hour.

Final word? There is nothing rational about the trimesters. You can categorize these nine (actually ten!) months under these cutely named umbrellas as I've done here, but that won't change the reality of it. Each stage is just that—a stage. You will cry, crave, and consume retail items you don't need. Just try and enjoy it for what it is: a process with some hip lingo.

11

WHOEVER SAID "LESS IS MORE" WASN'T PREGNANT

(SHOPPING DELIGHT)

Anyone who's experienced Black Friday shopping knows how completely insane it is. People pack whistles, snacks, even adult-sized diapers, and camp out to obtain the item they want. It's brutal. . . but shopping for your first baby's arrival is like thirty Black Fridays rolled up together.

Once again, social media messes with our notion of what shopping for a baby is. It imagines you looking immaculately fantastic in smart-casual linen, your hair perfectly wavy, strolling hand in hand with your partner who is also in linen. You're fingering onesies with a giant smile on your face as you contemplate the bundle of joy you're about to welcome who will sleep through the night (as long as you buy the right baby cot or co-sleeping basket). You giggle and hum Leonard Cohen's "Hallelujah" and talk about nothing other than how blessed you are.

It might be that way for you—and to that I will say I'm happy for you. I am. And again, no judgment. But, if we want to be really honest here, shopping for your firstborn is more like standing in IKEA sobbing about how you want to throw up because it smells like fungus-filled toes and because you don't know where product K53 is so you buy a lot more than you need. I mean, who really needs six mini chalkboards, countless bath toys, and three cots? *Three?* The only reason you can tell me to shut up is if you're having triplets. And that's roughly one in every sixty-seven pregnancies.

So, I am now living in a phase of panic involving major credit card debt and *maybe* over-shopping. Well, isn't that kind of the same thing? Ohhh, the story of my life. I remember when I had just moved to New York City, excited to be an adult. (I had finished my masters in England and had locked down in New York. It sounds much more impressive than it actually was.) I lived in a loft studio where you could brush your teeth, pee, and warm your cup of coffee all within a three-foot radius. It was small and I mean small, but I could afford it on my own so I loved it. And wait, please take a moment and erase all the *Sex and the City* imaginings from your mind because it actually wasn't like that at all. At least not for me. And if it was for you then I'm sure that's why we weren't friends.

My not-so-proudest moment was when I lived on popcorn. Umm, let's just say it was for more than a weekend. Well, popcorn and leftover sandwiches. Don't worry though, the sandwiches were from meetings I was called in for . . . most of the time. I became shameless at stuffing extra ones in my handbag to eat later and got better and better at doing it without making eye contact with anyone for fear of judgment. I also got better at wrapping them in enough tissue that they didn't spill all through my bag. These life skills really do come in handy once you start having kids.

Here's a list of things I learned about popcorn during my popcorn cleanse because I wanted to buy things other than food. Okay, so it was less of a cleanse, more of an ohmygod-this-is-the-cheapest-yummiest-thing-I-can-eat-right-now.

1. Popcorn is the official snack of Illinois. They even have an annual Popcorn Day. I don't understand why every nation doesn't have this as part of their social agenda?
2. Orville Redenbacher, the inventor of popcorn, started growing popping corn in 1919 when he was twelve years old. What were you doing when you were twelve? I mean, other than still picking your nose?
3. A cup of plain popcorn contains just thirty-one calories and about 953 with that cheese you like to put on it. (Fact-check this: I doubt it's true—I just wanted to make sure you're paying attention.)

Fast-forward a few years and I'm back in Dubai probably picking out a few kernels from my teeth (popcorn is just the perfect snack, pregnant or not!). Here I am standing in a store asking someone to help me. As in, helllppppp me. Okay, it was a little more italicized than that. *Helllppppp me.* Shopping in month three of pregnancy versus shopping in your last trimester is drastically different. In month seven, I'm standing in an awkward position with most things clenched because I don't want to let anything slip out. That's the majority of what you do your whole last trimester, actually.

Your basket looks like the whole store threw up in it. Burp cloths and onesies, socks and undershirts. Why the hell are there so many pieces and all are so tiny? How the hell am I going to fit someone into all this? Or rather, how the hell is someone going to fit into all of this without me breaking her?

I don't know why, but for some reason I couldn't stop myself from buying too many things. Or fifty-six of the same thing—burp cloths. Why do we do this? Was I in complete denial about the baby eventually having to come out? Maybe that's it. I wanted to keep this baby in—forever.

Here's how you know you are—as I was—in complete denial about the baby eventually having to come out:

1) How you talk about your summer plans:
   a) Words like "yacht," "four-day hike," and "wakeboarding" roll off your tongue. You talk about June being the perfect time to do all of this, which happens to coincide with your delivery date.
   b) You're planning on relying on www.lastminute.com, you know, last minute. Anyway, you can't go far or you'll have to figure out if there is a plug adapter for your bottle sterilizer.
   c) You know you'll be somewhat homebound with a photoshoot for the baby in the early days involving tons of hats and things to fit them in. You can't wait.

2) How you discuss how you chose a name:
   a) Whose name?
   b) Yeah, still deciding . . . I guess we'll figure it out when we meet him/her.

     c) You show your shortlisted top five and ask for a group vote.

3) As soon as you go on maternity leave from work you:
     a) Decide this is the perfect month to finish that poetry collection you were working on in college.
     b) Yeah, you'll probably figure out which room the baby can bunk in, to start with. Maybe paint, or scrap that, ask your dad-in-law to paint. He's handy.
     c) Got it all mapped out. You are organized and have notebooks for things.

Mostly As: Complete denial
Mostly Bs: You're not in denial, but you are still procrastinating on actual baby logistics and why would that be, girl? Hhhhmmmm?
Mostly Cs: You are with it, girl. Totally realistic and logical. I wanna be your friend. Also, I'm kinda jealous.

I know why I bought fifty-six burp clothes. It's because it's all I remembered from the list of essentials my sister barked at me—I'd left the printed-out list (one of the many typical pregnant brain fails) at home, so instead of procuring a range of requirements I remembered that one item too many times. Why are burpies not called vomit cloths? It's not like we catch burps in them. I mean, really, let's just call a spade a spade.

The minute I told my sister I was pregnant she also went through her depot and pulled out a whole bunch of things I probably didn't need. Did I want to buy my baby new things that were overpriced that I probably didn't need? Of course. Did I end up *also* taking my sister's rejects? Of course not. Take it all. Bicycle with three wheels? Take it. You're not breeding the next Lance Armstrong, are you? And in the meantime, you will save big by reusing other people's stuff at no cost to you. This is particularly great for toys because newborns are literally just as happy with a wooden spoon as a three-hundred-dollar rattle—if not more. This is normal. You are normal. So, we just have to expect the worst, hope for the best, and be open to everything—but not so open we go into premature labor in Baby Gap.

I quickly realized that I was going to have to be okay with owning fifty-six burp clothes and still have no clue which cot, stroller, or bottle sanitizer to buy. Most of all, though? I was going to have to be okay with to-do lists that never end and a very probable fair chunk of change in credit card debt. Long gone were the NYC days where I would try and pay for essential work wardrobe items at Bloomies and hold my breath as they swiped the card. That was illogical spending and debt no one would reprimand me for. This was much worse because I'm an adult who should have her act together enough to buy the basic, necessary baby needs. And yes, your baby has ears and can hear everything by now so let's hope his or her first words aren't, "Try and swipe it again?"

Best Friend or Archenemy?

Regardless of where you're from or what hair product you absolutely cannot live without, you are undeniably one massive messy hormone by now. Congrats. You can no longer hold your pee at all or elegantly wipe the sweat from your upper lip. And no one finds these facts the least bit cute or endearing. Not anymore. We've all been there where we've felt frazzled and short-tempered. Pregnant or not, we've all had to tap into our inner higher-self and light that lavender branch in chant. We have. Let's not deny it. Are you nodding yet? Let's leave the denial bit to the other mommy bloggers, influencers, and Instagrammers out there. I really do wanna try and keep things real. Like, really real. Relatably-real.

It's in the last trimester that other pregnant mamas and new mamas who are way sleep deprived will categorize you as either their new best friend or archenemy. I'm not gonna lie, it's harsh. It's like that scene from *Charlie and the Chocolate Factory* where Veruca Salt is in the egg room with all the eggs and Willy Wonka tells her most things get weighed like this—as a good egg or a bad egg—when Veruca gets sent down the garbage chute. Pregnant mamas do this. Mamas definitely do this. Wait, aren't most things measured like that, though?

I've been recently obsessed with observing how mamas behave when at the check-out counter in the hopes of befriending some before Gnocchi arrives. I'm like that hidden camera there to catch embarrassing and less-than-composed moments. I've actually caught myself mid eye-roll and deep sigh when the barely out-of-college cashier refuses to exchange a scarf covered in ducks that I was gifted last Christmas. Big shout out to my MIL—it's always the thought that counts—because the item almost always really sucks. There are a few different types of mamas I've been weighing up as bad or good eggs. Not judging, just observing and weighing. Again, not judging.

There are the ones trying to exchange an item bought eons ago (like me) or use a voucher for another store (that had since shut down) which is always fun.

There's also the one who darts off to grab a few last-minute items. She also unloads her entire purse on the carousel to find her wallet, leaving the queue gaping at the number of crumbs and chewed-candy-encrusted raisins rolling around with her iPhone, receipts, LEGOs, and My Little Ponies. Nowadays as a mama to three puzzle pieces, she's the one I'd be grabbing a glass of red and a few hand rolls of sushi with on Tuesdays.

And then there are the equipped few, with a list, an agenda, and a pair of comfy shoes to walk quickly and get things done. Her children are not with her. She is judged. She is hated. She is no one I know. Nope, not even from high school or work. Not even from Facebook or LinkedIn as someone you might congratulate on their work anniversary. She is an illusion and what I call the Unholy Triple U: the unattainable, the unrealistic, and the unachievable. Amen.

Needless to say, there is quite the beautiful rainbow of different mamas out there, and chances are if they're being a bit psychotic or are in headless-chicken mode, please . . . please don't gawk because you're probably staring at one of my besties . . . umm, or me. Just smile and maybe promise her things will get better. You never know if she's had a bad morning dealing with a colicky newborn, a shitty four-year-old, a grumpy toddler, or an even grumpier MIL who keeps asking why she's not wearing that duck scarf gift. Seriously, who wears silk scarves anymore?

When you are mama-watching and deciding if she's a bad or good egg, I don't mean bad or good as in ISIS or Mother Teresa, I mean bad or good as in, Can I be friends with this woman or not? Is she someone I want to text during my binges on mozzarella sticks dipped in hummus? It comes down to asking yourself whether or not she will smash your ego like a nutcracker. You know, your ever-so-fragile pregnant ego that can easily be crushed if someone offers you some under eye cream recommendations or suggests "the best antiperspirant that's still ecologically created."

So, despite the fact that there are these strange species called "SUPA-MAMAS" that's right, SUPA not SUPER because we all know misspelling things is a way to sound cool, these supa-mamas roam the earth making it all look way too easy and really annoying the crap out of the rest of us.

Being half Lebanese (as I'm sure I've said on more than a few accounts), I feel like a large chunk of my journey in mommyhood ought to focus on not only befriending but also becoming a supa-mama, which, again definitely hasn't worked out that way. Sure, I try to keep up my mani-pedis, but it hasn't been enough to put me on the archenemy list, nor have I worn enough track pants with yogurt-stained shirts to put me up there on the bestie list. So, where has that left me? I guess I want to be on both lists?

This idea of the supa-mama, though. It's fake. It's fabricated. It's bullshit. Why, you say? You don't agree? You wanna tell me all about that one stunning woman at the grocery store who you saw buying fresh kale and looking all put together with a small smile pursed on her lips like she can't wait to see just how perfect her delivery is going to be? Well, trust me, that woman is probably as constipated as you are, and the smile is trapped wind, or one of those bitter smiles over the latest passive-aggressive text war she's having with her husband. And that kale? This is the third bunch she buys this week. She swears she's going to eat it for the baby this time.

So, I've decided to aim to be supa-mama *some* of the time. The rest of the time I'll just watch KIA commercials and sob. I've had *moments* where I've felt like a supa-mama in the making. Moments where my nail polish hasn't chipped, where I've ordered the "right" thing for my baby off the menu, a brief flickering moment where I played classical music in my bathroom instead of Drake so my unborn child would emerge supa-smart . . . overall, though? I'm somewhere in the middle of that scale. Hate me if you want, but fast-forward to my third pregnancy where you will see me busy at the MAC counter sampling concealers on my varicose veins. That definitely categorizes me as a bestie, doesn't it?

Pincushion for Needles Part 1: The Gestational Diabetes Test

Why didn't anyone warn me how many times I'd be pricked and prodded and have samples of bodily fluids taken from so many places on my body? No one told me. I hate that. I mean, at least warn me. And this whole thing about the gestational diabetes test at around thirty-two weeks when you can barely ingest an apple because there's a tiny human sitting on your bladder and elbowing your stomach or whatever other organs she's pushing aside . . . yeah, not cool.

I absolutely hate blood tests (although to be honest, who loves them?) and hospitals, too. No, like a lot. I'm a bit envious of the unhygienic but homey locations our grandmothers used to give birth. Usually in the hallway or kitchen while stirring the gruel or something. I'm sure not many people were on anxiety medication because, well, they didn't exist. Plus, people just had to deal with whatever and not get upset. Oh, and they had to love the worst-case scenario, too. A useful skill I'm still trying to perfect. (Credit to my big brother for that one.) So, for me, my hatred of hospitals really all goes back to one doctor misdiagnosing a sinus infection for a brain tumor.

I was getting ready to compete in a track-and-field tournament in Rhodes, Greece when I had this crazy headache. It was like there was a 1950s iron inside my head slamming my skull like it was a 1950s ironing board. Not like, Oh, I have a headache let me pop a few Advil and get on with my day. No, like, let's call in the head of neurosurgery and see why half of her face is numb. Yes, I googled. Yes, WebMD become my homepage, and yes, my brother was on speed-dial. He was in his last year of medical school and was probably thinking the worst because he was studying it twenty-four seven. I hope he was finally feeling bad for those Monopoly torture sessions.

The doctor in Rhodes made the mistake of going from 0 to 100 in a second. Perhaps he could have done a few more tests before talking about chemo? I ended up being fine and after more than a few blood tests, a spinal tap, and more than a few MRIs I was sent to an ENT who gave me some hardcore meds (also known as saline solution or salty water) to be shot up my nose fifty-six times a day. And so the combination of my fear and hatred of hospitals culminated in me almost tipping over the edge that day of the gestational diabetes test, with screaming babies in every corner. Anyways, that's another book. Sequel to this one? Write in to my publisher and ask when my follow-up is slated to release?

So, this gestational diabetes test. Little did I know it takes me three to four hours and that I would have to sit there starving hungry from the overnight fasting, and have some blood drawn, then wait, then drink something so disgusting you want to retch—this something is an Orangina knock-off from a factory with no limits on the sucrose button—then have some more blood drawn, then wait some more, then have a bit more blood drawn (just for fun at that stage, I swear). And as if all that wasn't annoying enough, I didn't bring a book to read or any form of entertainment. I called my husband begging him to come by for a quick chat.

Me: Hi, baby! (excited and hopeful).

Mr. Excel: Hey, uh, babe (distracted and around work colleagues so must resort to calling me babe and refrain from calling me baby otherwise his masculinity would be questioned).

Me: Soooo, (trying to appear casual) I'm hanging out here getting this diabetes test thingy done and I have to stay another two hours to drink this liquid and then... (trying to make it sound more exciting than it is while also sounding like a bit of a sad puppy to score some sympathy points and get him to drive over to me with a chocolate muffin and a hot coffee to consume when this is all over and hoping he just read my mind to know all of that).

Mr. Excel: Is this urgent? I'm stepping into a meeting.

Me: Oh, okay . . . sure . . . yeah, well, I'll be here in case you wanna chat. Or check up on me. Or . . . do we have plans tonight by the way because I was thinking . . .

Mr. Excel: Yeah, that sounds good. See you tonight.

[Click]

Ouch.

After all was said and done (kinda hate that expression but it works as a transition here so spare me the lecture), that gestational diabetes test changed me.

I entered an even harder stage of being a pregnant woman. It can last for weeks on end and common symptoms are sobbing, yelling, and sudden urges to remove all your clothes and break out into a heat rash.

I got it now. This was big. These tests, the results . . . everyone's reaction and constant checking in on you. I was going to have to learn to be responsible and keep stuff together in a file and label it and not lose interest. Wait, wasn't that my forte though? The organizational part, yes, but the not-losing interest? I was like Dori in *Finding Nemo* with a three-second memory and lots of energy. A definite recipe for mini mess-ups along the way.

The good news was that I didn't have gestational diabetes. The bad news was that I was about to be a human pincushion again. I had to start thinking about dress fittings for that same brother who tortured me with the lamb's brain and made me obsess over Monopoly. Yes, he was getting married, and I had to find something to make me look like I had everything under control—bump, imminent birth, and a charming belly laugh to boot.

Pincushion for Needles Part 2: The Dress Fitting

Akh. Shopping for a dress when you feel gross and have to look cute especially for a family wedding and no, not a distant cousin's, but your very own brother. It's womanly nature (is that even a term?) to want to look your best at your siblings' weddings. But it's rarely realistic when they go down during a third trimester.

My sister was eight months' pregnant at my wedding (she has the poofy hair in all the family photos to prove it) and I am going to be around the same stage when my brother gets married. I'm not sure if that's really a sign or just a funny bonding experience we all have about wanting to look super-hot and coming across looking just that way in the photos. As in, overheated.

Finally, you spend way more than you wanted to on a dress that makes you feel kinda okay. I mean, it's better than gross. My go-to power color has always been red. Ever since a fortune-teller told me so ages ago. I vividly remember him positioning the Arabic coffee cup and studying coffee smears that stained the white cup only to conclude I had masculine energy and that red would balance my life out. Wait, or was it blue? Crap. Well, one of those, but my dress was red so red it was.

Before I knew it, I was dressed and talking to people about my older brother and how I would continue to be that annoying baby sister even after becoming a mama. People annoyingly warned me not to hit the dance floor too hard because the hospital was apparently an hour away. "You're exhausted from the belly bump and the wedding prep? Just waitttt, this is nothing," was heard while I took my fill of coconut shrimp. Three shrimps. I mean, at least let me enjoy my third-to-last month of life without baby before you whip out your phone to show me a high-def video of your vaginal birth and remind me to "TURN ON THE SOUND, THOUGH." And, no, I don't want to hear how much C-sections actually hurt, either. Just let me live happily in the land of "That's coming later," at least for a little bit. At least while I'm still trying to rock this Grecian-goddess-in-red look. *Trying* is the key word and I have to interject here and let you know that I felt, really felt, ugly at my brother's wedding, and possibly rightly so because I have the photos to prove it. No, like I was sick of my face. All of it. And what was going on with my eyebrows? It seemed like I was growing hair everywhere except where I needed it—on my head. But that's always the case, isn't it? These are the kind of superficial, completely self-loathing thoughts that take over my mind and in the next five seconds comes a flood of self-loving thoughts. It's really been quite an exhausting journey and the bulk of the exhaustion has been all mental. No wonder I started a blog. And drink a lot of coffee.

What's more, the grossness you feel when out in public at something like a family wedding is somehow proportional to how little sympathy you will get from people. So of course, I had to pass by Teta on my way to the dance floor where she shouted what she thought was a whisper, "I know you're not on your way to the dance floor because that would be a disgrace. Don't you dare make that baby dance. I'm too tired to go to the hospital for your birth tonight." Godfather style. I still hit the dance floor but avoided the outside of the dance circle where she could spot me and stare me down to my seat. Thank God my mom saw and told me "*yalla* enough . . .

last song I swear Haram . . . you're making her tired in there," while touching my belly. She said this while my dad motioned me over to ask me to make him a few fruit plates for his table. Weren't there waiters for that, Daddy?

Actually, the more disgusting it is for you to be pregnant, the more everyone else seems to blame you. That's right: Your suffering somehow signals others that you're violating your end-of-pregnancy social contract, which includes making sure being pregnant looks 100 percent joyful. It's really not all bad. The fullness, the kicking. There is a kind of serene self-containment that comes with it, and at times it can feel like femininity in bloom. But then everything aches and you catch a glimpse of your back acne and the grossed-out glow returns. Just like that. As if you had willed it.

12

YOU SAY HOMiCiDAL, i SAY HORMONAL

(HOW DARE YOU SAY "GOOD MORNiNG" TO ME?)

You've given up trying to find cute things to wear. You now do everything in tights pulled down under the bump and one of your husband's shirts. It kinda works but then you FaceTime your best friend and she tells you it doesn't. You cry when he asks you why you're wearing his shirt. You accuse him of cheating and of not loving you because if he was faithful and really truly loved you he would let you wear his shirt and not ask questions. No one understands you. And you can't understand why you never have any cold Chinese noodles in the fridge when everyone *knows* that's all you want. It's not just the way he blinks that makes me angry. I think I'm just generally more annoyed since getting pregnant. Especially so in the last trimester. I'm over it. Over the research and the worry and the excitement and the ohhhh is this meat well-done? And the endless asking if that parsley touched the fish I'm about to consume and calculating from what body of water the fish is from and with what level of mercury. I want and need sushi.

Getting carried away is regular fallout in pregnancy. I was *emotional*. When you're pregnant and about to be a new mom you don't need a song to come on the radio to make you cry. I would cry for no reason and crying for no reason didn't compute for Mr. Excel, so finally I would make something up, as in, "I'm crying because we don't have any mustard." Men need reasons and explanations. The correlation between my pregnancy and his extended "workload" was too perfect to be anything but a bid to escape his crazy pregnant wife.

I've decided to try and work through these things on my own and kinda made a list of things that have gotten under my skin these last few months:

1. Why the grilled fish has way too much or not enough lemon. And tabouleh is a toxo-immune's nightmare with all that parsley.
2. Other people's whiny kids asking for five more minutes.
3. My mother in law's perfume, mostly because it's the same one my mom uses.
4. The fact that my mom answers the phone like she doesn't have caller ID and know who I am.
5. Random advice from cashiers: "Popcorn again? You buy carrot also."
6. Static on the radio.

What else? Gosh, there are honestly way too many to list here. I feel really bad for my husband because well, I have to say I have a good one. I really do. I mean we should really compete on those game shows where couples get asked who knows who better . . . I bet we'd win. Or come in second place. Or we'd talk about how we would totally win this show from the comfort of our couch in comfy pj's with the AC on way too strong. Yeah, that sounds more like us.

So, half the time I can't decide what I want to have for dinner, let alone decide if I actually love him or hate him this morning. You see, it fluctuates. It just does. Like most things in pregnancy, actually. Up and down then down and back up again. Needless to say, I do feel bad for hating my husband lately.

It's not that I don't love him anymore or anything ridiculous like that, it's really much simpler—I just can't stand the sight, smell, or touch of him. Like, at all. No, not even when he shows off his understated dimple and charming chocolate brown eyes. There is no charm, sparkle, attraction, or humor when you're eight months' pregnant. There just isn't. Fact. Why does this happen to us right before a new entity is introduced into our marriage? Sure, you can read a ton of books about babyproofing your marriage and keeping the mojo alive and all that, but does any of it actually work? No, that's not what I mean to ask. What I mean to ask is do you actually implement any of it?

Exactly.

I'm a bit all over the place with how I feel about this pregnancy. I'm over it and over the millions of questions from the thousands of relatives I get on a daily basis over the hundreds of ways we all communicate. I'm sure things were much, much easier in the eighties. No need to be so dramatic, Actually, I'm sure things were much, much easier in the nineties. You know, BS (before social).

The Vibe Door-Card

As you can tell by now I've included a bunch of these mini quizzes to reassure you that you can do no wrong as a pregnant mama-to-be. You're growing a human being and that's sacred. So, to shake things up a little, here's one for your beloved life partner. A mini quiz you can fill in and hang outside your door to give your partner a heads-up on what sort of vibe they are walking into:

1. You find your old wedding photos and immediately:
   a) Kiss each and every one of them and think wow, I didn't think it would be possible that I would or could ever love him more. You do, and that's MAGICAL. Cue the imagined whinnying of unicorns.
   b) Wonder why you've both gained so much weight. Oh, that's right. You're pregnant. What's his excuse? Google map nearby "ex-military personal trainers" and book him in for Ironman training tomorrow morning.
   c) Ask yourself what you were thinking. How could you have said yes? How are you now having a baby with this person? Who is he? I mean, do you even know each other? You start packing toiletries (without a plan) muttering, "What was I thinking? Godddddd."

2. The topic of naming the baby comes up, you:
   a) Hold your husband's hand lovingly and use "we" at the start of every sentence. You start to sound like you're speaking French you say "we" so much.
   b) Roll your eyes and say, "Let's go through our list again? Mmmmhhhh? Don't worry, you'll get your head around my favorite top three, honey. It just takes some effort on your part."
   c) Slap your forehead, Skype your mom and his into a group call, and start screaming, "OHMYGOD, telllllllll themmmm what you want to name her. Tell them. IS AVATAR EVEN A NAME?"

3. Your hubby calls you from work to ask what you want for dinner. Your response:
   a) "Anything you want, baby. You know, our little one has the same exact taste buds as you." (Giggle as he says something along the lines of "that's maboy.") Chicken wings it is. Screw nutrition.
   b) "Ummm, I don't know. I can't decide. I'm still kinda annoyed that you ordered pizza yesterday when you know tomato sauce makes me gag. But it's okay. For now."
   c) "Is that some sort of a trick question? Is this your way of telling me that you want me to order something? Wait, wait, wait, you're expecting me to cook something? Is this all a code for something? Do you want a divorce? Are you calling me fat?"

Mostly As: Come in. It's safe. It's more than safe. You just may get lucky tonight, that is, if you can manage to block out hearing her say, "Sorry, baby but this won't take long. Daddy just needs a minute."

Mostly Bs: It could be safe. Or not. Nothing is really clear except the fact that this is a gray zone. Not a war zone or a green zone or a humanitarian zone, but as gray as setting concrete. Advice: Stick to what you know and use a maximum of three to five words when speaking to her.

Mostly Cs: Go get a beer with your friends. No hesitation. Like maybe for a week or two. But don't you dare look happy about it because that will call for some lawyering up.

Avoid Anyone with a Real Baby

I have a close friend of mine in Dubai who's actually one of the most calm, collected, and rational women I know. Very rarely does she have a freakout moment. Having said that, I went to visit after she was back from delivering in New York and discovered a somewhat changed woman. Long gone was my overly composed and border-line freakishly CALM friend and what had replaced her was a some-what less calm and collected woman with a three-month-old baby attached to the end of her arm. He was beyond cute and she was beyond exhausted. I barely entered her apartment and she grabbed my arm with a death grip. I had never in my life had my arm pinched so hard and felt so panicky myself at the thought of someday being in her place. I scurried out after reassuring her that I was sure things would get better, easier, and be wonderfully romantic like all of those diaper commercials.

It would seem logical to have things center around you, right? Yes, I totally agree. Friendships change, and I have definitely stopped calling the friends who are singletons and still doing shots and sim-ilarly, the phone calls have definitely stopped from those who have teenaged kids. Yes, I will be there one day, but not today. And until I'm there I only want to wave to you. From way over here. I want to stay in my ignorance-is-bliss state of being for as long as I can.

Pass Me Another Twig, Will You?

Okay, so it is clearly *not* a cliché that pregnant women should not handle heavy machinery, be in charge of grocery shopping, and be held accountable for any of their behavior while pregnant, or even during breastfeeding, and perhaps throughout the entire duration of motherhood. Yes, the nesting instinct is also a certainty in preg-nancy. Just as you see birds making their nests, mothers-to-be do exactly the same. There seems to be no end to the lengths a nesting mother will go. Feng Shui, Mommy. Feng Shui.

I have spent the last five years of my life being the aunt, and the friend who's supportive of pregnancy. The girl who oohs and ahhhs and shrieks at the sight of a toe on the ultrasound. I was officially and completely that girl. It has been fun and exciting but most of all educational. I have been making mental notes along the way of things I would want to do exactly the same way and, similarly, things I would want to do completely different. Creating a spreadsheet of items that must be bought, and budgeting expenses were just some of the things on my to-do list. Getting inspired by Pottery Barn catalogs was also key, as was reorganizing my closet and rearranging everything by color until suddenly realizing I have nothing to wear (since nothing fits anymore) and then realizing there's stuff in there that's kind of old. Old and doesn't fit? This bothers me, so I must spend the next five hours completely reorganizing it. Who cares if my back is hurting? This has to be done tonight. Like NOW.

As with animals in the wild, the pregnant human female will one day have the uncontrollable urge to get her little nest in order. I kept reading about this and thinking, "When is my instinct going to kick in?" Well, it kicked in on overdrive and was coupled with a cleaning urge. I wanted everything to be perfectly placed and in the cleanest manner. It was more than nesting, it was obsessive compulsive disinfecting. Definitely do not try and stop yourself from taking part in the nesting instinct and muttering "That doesn't go *there* that goes *there*" while walking around your house. You become obsessed with adjusting those twigs. It's okay. They're just "twigs."

13

WHAT GOES iN MUST COME OUT

(ALL THE UNIVERSAL TRUTHS YOU COULD EVER WANT)

Governments should invest in an international pregnancy policy where there are indestructible rules about people who pat your stomach, give you unsolicited advice about giving birth, or talk to you of nothing but your condition. Yes, condition and state of being. This really should be written down—not just "understood" like those understood policies, you know the ones: "daddy gets the biggest piece of chicken" and birthdays start at midnight. What, you don't know that one? No, not the time you were born (one o'clock in the afternoon in my case) or the very next morning. Mr. Excel and I have fought about this again and again so to all the partners out there I would like to say consider this an unbreakable rule, understood? *Birthdays start at midnight.* At 12:01 a.m. the fireworks should go off.

This policy would also forbid complete strangers, or friends, or your uncle's wife, and most of all anyone from your husband's side of the family from asking you questions that are too in-depth or probing. Just, stop. Similarly, there should be a penalty placed on those who offer up old rubbish about how they found childbirth completely pain-free. That's nice. For you. You are clearly a person who has erased all memories of pain. Or were you knocked out on chloroform?

As our designated driver of this new preggopolicy, Sweden, I'm looking at you. Step up your game. With child allowance for all families no matter the household income, free schooling, free public transport for any adult with a stroller, 480 days of paid parental leave, come on, Sweden, who gave us *Mama Mia* the Musical, Baby Bjorns, Spotify, that's it?

Name the Celebrity Who Called Their Baby Kumquat

Baby showers. You either hate them or love them. Yes, kinda like Vegemite. I've never actually tried Vegemite but that's what people say so I'll steal that analogy and spread it thinly here. So, I decided not to have one. And before you ask whyyyy . . . there were and still are lots of reasons. It was complex and would have been filled with frills—two things I am absolutely allergic to. My general take on the baby shower, though? Exploit it. You can get almost all the gear you need for the baby's first two years of life in terms of gadgets and clothes. Exploit away and keep those receipts. You're going to be invited to a whole bunch of baby showers and nothing's better than exchanging and re-gifting. Just be aware you can only do that so many times before you will be busted. And being busted for re-gifting at a baby shower has a particularly bad vibe to it.

And now for an essential quiz to let you know what type of person you are at baby showers (as if you didn't know already).

1. The games begin (you know the ones I'm talking about—match each celebrity to their baby's ridiculous name. Which celebrity named their baby Kumquat again?) You immediately:
   a) Sheepishly smile, think *awwww,* and get ready to snap a few pictures so the mama-to-be can remember this forever. You also make sure to catch her in some good lighting.
   b) Roll your eyes but grit your teeth and remind yourself this isn't about you. If you have kids, this is a non-boozy escape from them, and if you don't have kids yet, this is the perfect time to make a list of what you do and do not want at your future baby shower. Lame doilies? Definitely no.
   c) Roll up your sleeves to get ready to get down and dirty. Who invented the pacifier? You know the answer and you're not afraid to push your neighbor aside and blurt it out. You're in it to win it. And who cares if winning it

means you get a free package of diapers when you don't even have a boyfriend let alone a baby? You'll take it. Winning is winning.

2. Every baby shower is awkward for the oversharing. How do you deal:
   a) Hug whoever is across from you and offer either encouragement or open up on all the awful parts of your own life.
   b) Cut them off by saying one of the following, depending on what they said: "Oh so cute." Or, "We've been so busy with our amazing careers and traveling." Or, "Yeah . . . I'm super picky, too."
   c) Counter attack everything with a smile and the following lines: "Yeah my kids are gonna be mixed race . . . for sure they will get poached by model agencies but yours could also be cute with better lighting." Or, "Do you really think your marriage is gonna last? How often do you have sex?" Or, "Sure he looks nice. No, for sure he's into you."

3. What gift do you bring to a baby shower?
   a) The onesie box set with the tiny socks and gloves that everyone coos over. It is the class gift. The much-needed item and the branded one. This baby will be rocking Ralph Lauren thanks to you.
   b) A massage for the mama-to-be because practical is your thing. She'll get enough onesies for sure.
   c) A checklist of milestones and what your baby should be doing when because that's the only way to win. And life is all about winning.

Mostly As: You're that genuine, uncompetitive friend. You can be present and detach from any other voice inside your head because you are so busy being in the moment.

Mostly Bs: You are silently competitive. Meeting a mom of four immediately causes you to make a mental note to yourself to eventually have five. I mean, after getting married. I mean, once you meet the right guy.

Mostly Cs: Okay so you're a tad bit inappropriate. Yup, you're that friend. Enough said. Glad they all talked you out of getting her a stripper pole for "fitness purposes" post-delivery. Wait, they didn't? It's being set up for her in her lounge during the shower? You didn't.

It's Babe O'clock

Before you know it you're almost in the home stretch. What else do you have to do? Where was that list? Where was that crucial Post-it with that one thing you scribbled on it that you had to do . . . or not do? And then there is the guilt of a pedicure. I am by no means a lazy and self-indulgent individual. However, like most Lebanese I do enjoy the typical manicure-pedicure. Today, I experienced guilt for the first time ever for having my toes painted. My sister called me and rattled through her day, which consisted of diarrhea, puking, no sleep, Sharpie-drawn-on furniture, someone eating a crayon, and a husband working late. When she finished she took a breath and said, "How're you doing?" I didn't have the heart to tell her absolutely amazingly relaxed, so I said, "Ohhh you know same old heartburn and inability to sleep." It would have been convincing except for the fact that Josie had just decided to start my foot massage at that moment and so what I wanted to convey as nonchalant ended up sounding drugged up. But, then again, I was allowed, wasn't I? No one said a foot massage wasn't allowed during the last month of pregnancy. Oh wait, they did? Crap. Ughhhh, add it to the list!

You might get one day of pampering before your due date. If you're lucky. Once the baby shower games are done, the pacifier cupcakes consumed, and that spa voucher used, reality sets in then. Reality sets in and you freak out. You stay up YouTubing videos of delivery options and somehow end up watching forest births and a C-section. The only thing that keeps you going is the thought of finally getting a bite of sushi and a sip of white wine when this is all over.

In my last week or so of being pregnant all I want is: a comfortable position. That's all. I really want nothing else. Nothing else at all. I'm stuck in a never-ending choose-your-own-adventure in which my choices are uncomfortable or even more uncomfortable, and yet I'm looking for a third hidden option to ideally cross a river and find that one magic cushion that will help me get some uninterrupted shut-eye. I really would be thankful for anything more than ten minutes. Beggars can't be choosers, right?

I always thought that the whole ohmygod-I-simply-can't-get-comfortable refrain was an act. That is, until that last week. Long gone are my days of jumping excitedly out of bed to choose an appropriate playlist to suit the day. My approach to the day involves a movement I refer to as the sloth-whale rollout. What playlists have I been choosing for Gnocchi to enjoy and start the day to? A compilation of swearing, grimacing, "ugh's," with a symphony of "oh shit's." Falling asleep is freaking impossible.

The to-do list is stressing me out. When does it all have to get done by again? What's my deadline? When's my due date? WAIT. Even though there are always sock drawers to organize, emotions to wrangle, money to save, bottle teats to sanitize, birthing bags to pack, and birth plans to tell your sister so she laughs so hard she falls off a chair, I implore you right now to stop and do the following things while you can: stare at a wall, do nothing, discuss your hair, phone a friend, for the love of god, sleep, go to the grocery store, and wander the aisles aimlessly.

Actually, that list's pointless. Scrap that. There's actually just one thing to do. Are you ready? *Close your eyes and just sit there for a minute.* There. That's it. Okay, a minute's done. Now carry on.

The Universal Truths to Keep

Whether it's via C-section or "down there." You did it. Or your doctor did. And a bit of the credit can be given to your baby, for sure. Throughout this memoir/journey/road trip minus the yummy snacks, I have tried to dismiss unnecessary rumors you as a first-time pregnant gal or Prega-Virgin (oxymoron, they need a cooler name for that) will come across, either through reading or from stories shared at five-hour gals' luncheons. I have attempted to keep it real and give off a relaxed and laidback yet not-in-total-denial feel to this book. Particularly for those of you that are newly pregnant.

But, here's the thing. No mama has the same pregnancy or delivery. Not one mother. Some are harder than others and some mamas face an unexpected turn of events where they have to accept and adjust to disappointment within a handful of seconds. Because birth plans do not always happen according to plan. Or you can have the perfect birth, but something goes down and . . . well, it's twelve days in neonatal intensive care. We all know accepting and adjusting can be the hardest things in life. All aspects of pregnancies and births are unknown.

Even if you always wanted kids, you still can't have much of an idea of what it will really be like to have a baby because there is no way to know without doing it. Sitting beside a real live baby just ain't the same. Even if you want to be pregnant, you can't know before-hand exactly how your body will react to the experience. The point is, a big part of pregnancy and parenting is out of your hands and that's not always a bad thing. That's really part of the fun—as trite or terrifying as that might sound to you now. Try as we might to control our fates, life socks us with the unforeseen on a regular basis.

Pregnancy instills an odd sense of excitement, panic, and fear, plus hope like how it felt right before we venture forth away from high school, or what it's like imagining what life will be like when we grow up. Know this: even if motherhood feels like it's *hurtling* at you through space with almost no time to prep, you actually don't need to get it all together. You learn on the fly.

Also, the role of "mother" may feel like the only "you" there is now, but it is merely one designation among many monikers in your life. It alone does not define you. Even if it's covered in clichés about mashed yams, turning lemons into lemonade, stepping up to the plate, being the best you possible, opening your heart up to love, and all that crap.

It really should be no surprise here that I've got a list for you now. I made lists for everything pre-birth. Items I still had to buy, things I had to do, the fact that I probably should be brushing my teeth daily, you know, the usual. And my favorite and possibly the most impor-tant of all: the universal truths that you will throw out the window. Also known as a mama's birth plan.

1. I wanted to deliver naturally. (I didn't.)
2. I didn't want an epidural. (Was I on crack? I *so* did.)
3. I wanted to breastfeed for a minimum of twelve months. (I did forty days. My MIL thinks I'm still breastfeeding all three

kids to this day. They are currently four years old, two years old, and sixteen months old.)

4.   I wanted my two closest girlfriends and my mom in the room with me with lavender scented candles. (Okay, not really, but it crossed my mind later until I remembered that it was so not my style. I had Mr. Excel there in scrubs looking a bit awkward.)

Seriously, I wanted to deliver naturally. I didn't want an epidural, and I thought I wanted to breastfeed for as long as the baby wanted. When my sister finally stopped laughing when I confided my birth plan and hopes and dreams to her, she said, "Unrealistic expectations in life are the biggest disappointments and GET DOWN FROM THAT CUPBOARD OR I SWEAR I WILL CALL THE POLICE TO TAKE YOU AWAY."

[Click]

She was right, because on day three after giving birth I would have paid a goat to milk me. But I didn't know that yet. When we heard that I would need a C-section to give birth to Gnocchi, my sister wasn't surprised that I was copying her again, and my brother loved the drama. It was surgery. A major operation. They would move my uterus aside or take it out of me for a bit. Like a magic trick or something.

I ate popcorn the night before the cut-off time of when I wasn't allowed to eat any more, and I remember being extremely thirsty but wasn't allowed to drink water after the cut-off time to avoid puking everywhere from the anesthetic and being unable to take one of those pictures where the baby is holding your pinkie. I have that photo in Gnocchi's first-year journal. I love that picture and what I wrote. "*Anyways, all stupid problems because I'm focused on you coming out healthy and happy. I can't believe that it's going to be one of the last times I feel you in my tummy. I feel a bit bad that you have no idea that they're going to pull you out today. You're like swimming away happily in there and someone is going to suddenly pull you out. We're ripping the Band-Aid off and getting right in there. I hope you love me as much as I'm going to love you and don't make too many stinky poopies.*" Little did I know that in the blink of an eye she would turn four and tell me that she didn't love me. I would sob in the bathroom but compose myself and respond with, "It's okay, it's not your job to love me. It's mine to love you." And that there would be countless varieties and bouts of diarrhea I would become a professional at dealing with—sometimes with a baby wipe shoved up my nose to block out the smell, but all from a place of love.

Giving birth? It was intense. It was different. It was overwhelming like a sudden case of food poisoning, only you are much happier. I didn't know it was going to be so hard. I didn't realize it would be like this. I wish my mom had warned me. These are all the expected things to say about giving birth.

I went into the operating room without contact lenses, jewelry, or makeup on (amateur mistake). I look as shell-shocked in the photos as Gnocchi does from being pulled out legs first. Before we knew it, we heard her cry and our life was complete. Ummm, let me just tell you, I didn't hear that cry, instead I was transfixed by the "burned skin" smell of my skin being cauterized and feeling major pressure in my abdomen as my doctor pushed organs back into their rightful place and complimented the muscle tone in my abs. Small talk or girl crush? Not sure.

In any small or large gathering of women, a camaraderie exists among those who have experienced childbirth. It's like a secret handshake or an ultraviolet mark detectable only to other moms. You will have that, and soon before you know it, you will have the ability and sleek skill to bond with other pregnant women and moms of any age from any ethnicity and with any number of kids to vent about.

This is that part of finding the magic in motherhood that instinctively brings out parts of you that you never knew existed. There's no #parentingfail on this one. Like a sudden light switch turned on, certain truths you weren't sure about suddenly shine in neon. You're a mom! Above all, you will come to terms with the fact that it's not all puppies and rainbows but is something that will bring out the A-game in you. Your birth story will be unique. As every mama's is. Welcome to mommyhood, can you smell the magic? Or is that meconium?

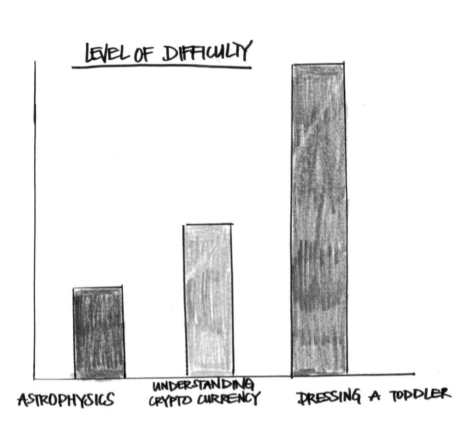

LEVEL OF DIFFICULTY

ASTROPHYSICS   UNDERSTANDING CRYPTO CURRENCY   DRESSING A TODDLER

BABY BOOTiE CAMP

It's crunch time. Game over. Whistle is blown and the fat lady has finished singing. You have been counting down to your baby's birthday like nothing before. Before you know it you will have filled your entire camera space with 164 photos of your baby yawning some with soft lighting and a different bib, of course. You have also dressed them in overly embarrassing outfits (no one wants to dress like a penguin when they're three weeks old, okay?). You think you're tired but you're not sure because it's all a haze. The emotions, the drooling (theirs and yours, too). It is all a bit too new and a bit too awkward and a bit too BPPM-filled. All in all, it's a lot of first time sorrys, whys, and I don't knows. Focus on what's good for the soul and get to know your "hood."

14

EAT, SLEEP, POOP, REPEAT

(HI THERE, WEREWOLF?)

Yes, mommyhood does reveal and expose parts you never knew existed. It brings out bits you forgot existed and exaggerates them. You quickly realize it's not all happy-go-lucky. It's more like paranoia and Ritalin. (For you, not your kids, obviously . . . at least not yet.) I say embrace the dysfunction and apprehension. Of. It. All.

The haze, oh, the haze of childbirth. I'm not sure if I can even call it that, seeing as I had a scheduled C-section. All I remember is being annoyed at Mr. Excel for not sitting near me, holding my hand, and gazing at me with pure awe and adoration. I had to ask if he felt okay. He was white although he did manage to snap a picture of me with the oxygen mask on. I was tied down—something I only realized later. Only much later did I learn they do this so you don't inadvertently reach out to grab your baby and mess up the sterile environment they've created for the surgery. Sure. And, yes, it is a creepy as it sounds if you haven't experienced it.

After some tugs and pulls, much like at the dentist's, numb but very much aware, Gnocchi was born. They plopped her white-gunk-covered body next to my face. It was intimate and etched in my mind like a permanent Etch A Sketch. I couldn't touch her, you know, my hands being tied down and all, but I did manage to rabbit kiss her (which made it look like I was sniffing her in the majority of our first pictures together).

Everyone is different and that's what makes us special. We all know this, thanks to our kindergarten teachers—and a big shout out to Mrs. Thomas for that and for not correcting my pencil grip—I still hold the pencil incorrectly. Wait, actually, just *differently* to 99.2

percent . . . okay, 99.9 percent of the population. I'm not sure if she passed over it and was too busy telling Stanley to stop picking his nose and pulling his pants down (something I vividly remember) or if she intentionally chose to let me express myself through gripping the pen like my life depended on it. Regardless, the outcome was the same—I hold pens a certain way, which turned out to be a great conversation starter and the root of many of my mom's lectures.

I guess everyone you meet deserves a different (not necessarily better or worse) kind of greeting but a different *unique* greeting all the same. Of all the profound things I had planned on saying to Gnocchi all I said was, "Hi." Hi? Not even a formal hello. I mean, after all, we were meeting for the first time, weren't we? Is this how guys feel after planning a suave line that comes out totally and utterly lame? My "hi" was a clumsy "pretttayyy" some dude says when ogling an attractive brunette with perfect waves. This "hi" though, was memorable. It opened the floodgates to a whole new dimension of love, lack of sleep, and worry.

Like hearing your baby's heartbeat—seeing them for the first time is a real moment. A moment where you realize life is about something other than checklists and achievements. That it's bigger than the stuff we worry about and get consumed by. It is the perfect reminder that there are 1,440 minutes in a day and let's all refuse to waste another 1/1,440 on anything as silly as whether or not you can pull off those leather pants. Well, at least not for the rest of *today*.

What went through my mind was that I'd changed it—my mind, that is. I wanted to keep her in utero. Permanently. Mainly because I didn't want to screw this up. Yup, I wanted to fill in *that* form. "One baby to stay inside for ten months possibly extending to a few years"—but it was too late. There was no possibility to undo what was born. Or rather, who was born.

When our little Gnocchi emerged her eyes were wide open as if to say, "Hey, what took you guys so long? What's the plan for the rest of the afternoon? I got bored in there!" Some babies are born yawning, ready to snuggle on the couch already. Others have an expression of discontent as if to say, "Where's my marching band? You guys need to step up your game." That was my second. I swear he was like, "For Chrissake stop taking pictures of my butt and roll out my red carpet already." And my third was like, "I'm going to be overly accommo-dating and smiley, a great eater and sleeper, and I will only poop in considerate places and never on the plane where the changing table is smaller than I am." We called him our unexpected surprise as a result of tons of red wine, but no regrets. He is our Grand Finale, at least that's what Mr. Excel keeps calling him to shut me up about the prospect of maybe-possibly-not-now-but-maybe-in-a-year having a fourth puzzle piece.

Gnocchi was just happy to be meeting new people. Her doctor, her nurse, and oh yeah, her parents. Okay, I know this next bit is going to sound like an acceptance speech at the Oscar's where the lead actress in a dramatic role is sobbing onstage showing way too much cleavage and leg. But I did warn you I'm dramatic like that. That day she also met *her* Teta (Grandma) who she would quickly develop a friendship with. It was a friendship based on whispered secrets at bedtime and giggles about pink eye shadow, midnight cookies, and fashion faux pas. Jiddo (Grandpa) Walid was at the hospital that day, too, and little did she know that he would be stuck on the same joke, "What does one wall say to the other?" and repeat that same joke over and over for a few years. "Meet me at the cor-ner." We know. I think he thought it would get funnier with time and when she could answer back. It hasn't. Gnocchi also had her first encounter with how dysfunctional my family and technology are when she watched me Skype my brother. It was basically a lot of yelling, bad angles, and an even worse connection. He started calling her Ice Cream that day for whatever reason, and I knew I had been replaced. My sister was there and would end up only having boys and would quickly begin a dance of adoration called girly sparkle for days. Basically, she bought Gnocchi everything girly—from dainty shoes when she could barely walk to sparkly nail polish and under-wear. Gnocchi's little boy cousins were also there and shoved roses into her little basket while asking endlessly if they could see how small her butt was. Gnocchi really was excited—or hungry. Now that I think about it she was probably hungry, but back then we took everything as excited.

Oh, yeah, and my in-laws called.

Let's dive into the part where I divulge about hospital stays in foreign countries. No, really. Let's. Little did I know that my Beirut hospital stay would be blissful. Beyond blissful. More like a mini vacation, really. Giving birth in Beirut was a bit of a political risk and yes, Lebanon gets a lot of things wrong with the electricity cuts, political instability, and lack of organization in almost everything, but still . . . my parents are there. My *mama* lives there. As if my mama wasn't enough, pampering-wise (possibly because of French colonization), the hospital has the babying thing down pat. Oh, not babying the babies, but the mamas, I mean. Jasmine tea and anise tea were served up that first night while the baby was whisked away to get cleaned and dressed. Not to mention a business card was left on my breakfast tray with a hairdresser's number who could come and sort my hair out before any pictures or visitors. Then, I hit day three and the baby blues. That is one massive ugly cry that lasts twenty-four hours.

So, yes, this sudden love for hospitals has come as a drastic shift from how I used to feel about hospitals when the baby was still in utero. Now that she's out, though? I look for that break. I now understand why my sister used to lick my mug rim right after I would tell her I had a confirmed diagnosis of bronchitis. I didn't think I would ever look forward to going to the dentist like I am excited for it now. Lying down and listening to a podcast or a bit of an audiobook? Yes, please! Oh, God, I hope I have a cavity and am not just going in for a twenty-minute clean.

Don't get me wrong. Hospital food is gross, the sheets not your own, and the bathroom doesn't have your scented candle's smell, but you have someone checking up on you. That role reversal is enough to make any mama wait in line at a curry food truck and pray to get the strain of food poisoning reported about in the news.

We need it to recuperate. Post-birth, pre-mama bootcamp with all the crazy colic and talk of who she looks like and why you're not giving her enough salmon. I call it practical. You're given a mini break for a few days before motherhood really begins i.e. when you're away from every single relative and when your mom has left and you're all alone staring at your two-week-old in desperate fear eyeing your tray of food where a wide selection of fenugreek and *meghli* (traditional Lebanese rice pudding spiced with anise, cinnamon, and caraway and garnished with shredded coconut and nuts) is served up. Both meant to increase milk production.

Having a newborn isn't so new to me now, having three puzzle pieces, but I'm always a little scared yet in love with the smell, booties, onesies, and hair, but mostly the smell. What is that? Cotton candy, hugs, and homemade bread? A newborn—after they're cleaned up, of course, because they're just gross before, honestly—smells of bliss. Like the last precious drops of your mom's perfume and freshly baked focaccia bread. Like those bakeries in NY where, when you walk past one you inhale as deep as possible to fill yourself up with that warm scent. She's everything good and soft and wondrous in the world. She's yours and you're excited—until she cries for absolutely no reason and you have no idea what to do. I'm always a little scared, too, by how weird newborns look. Yeah. That really freaky stuff. When you're thinking, "Wait, did I just give birth to a werewolf?" Here are seven critters from the animal world that you may be reminded of while gazing at your bundle of baby love:

1. Giant Black Slug: That first black poop with the consistency of tar and sounds like the word melatonin but isn't. Honestly, YouTube giant black slug and be disgusted.

2. Snake: The peeling-off skin thing. Like a whole layer. And, no, moisturizing doesn't help and you can't scrub, either.

3. American Eagle: That going-bald phase. I hated finding patches of my baby's hair in their crib, but it's part of the process and you might consider shaving their head to save them the embarrassing patchy look.

4. Toad: Those little white bumps that look like whiteheads which apparently are called milia, and I have no idea why they appear but they disappear in a few weeks. That's going to be a heck of a Photoshop job after the newborn photoshoot you have scheduled. Unless you apply cover-up?

5. Werewolf: Whether your baby has a full head of hair or is completely bald, there's a good chance they have some peach fuzz. The medical term for it is lanugo, and it's there to regulate the baby's body temperature in the womb or something like that. Whatever you do, don't break out a razor to get rid of it: it'll shed soon enough. Gnocchi had it on her ears. Avoid the light of a full moon if it's really bad . . .

6. Opossum: I'm sorry but they are . . . cross-eyed. At least in the beginning. A newborn's eyes don't always move in perfect unison. That off-kilter gaze is simply due to the fact that, like the rest of them, they are uncoordinated and need practice flexing those muscles. Still cute, though.

Next on your to-do list is sorting out your lovable werewolf's hair situation out. But, first? Spicy salmon rolls and a humongous gulp of white wine.

Your "I'm a Mom" Freak-Out

Much like your BPPM—your big psycho pregnancy moment— you'll have your "I'm a mom" mini-freak-out. Or maxi-freak-out. Your call. This may happen on day three when you have the baby blues. Or in week two or so when your mom/great aunt Martha/ Dutch *kraamzorg* leaves. Or when your partner has to return to work leaving you facing a newborn all day long alone. Your I'm-a-mom freak-out can be as simple as a love gush that you love every inch of this new person in your life and if it's not (mine wasn't) that's okay, too. Some have a Kenyan nanny who makes the best blueberry pancakes, or a sister who lives next door, or husbands who run their own businesses and are around the house more. It doesn't matter. The mathematical formula or equation is never the same, yet it always gives us the same answer—this mama needs her freak-out. There are exceptions, though, and if you don't have that moment then it just means it's pent-up inside you and will probably come out when your kids are going through their terrible twos. Or at high school graduation. Perfect.

This morning I caught myself. I am a mom. Officially. I left my apartment to take Gnocchi for a short walk. We got downstairs after squealing and singing "we're going outsideeeeeeeeeeeeeee" in the elevator with a guy on his way down to the gym. He was not amused. After we said good morning to everything and everyone in sight, we watched a construction worker saw down part of a tree and the birdies fly around. For an hour. She was all focused while I was WhatsApping ten minutes in.

I realized that there are several obvious ways to tell if someone is a mom or not:

1. You catch yourself exclaiming "This is a zipper!" To get her to stop crying. You spend long minutes showing her how one works, forgetting that you're flashing everyone your orange South Beach underwear.
2. You smell everything and anything for poo-poo.
3. At the very glimpse that someone looks remotely upset you immediately go in for a hug and say in a disgustingly coo-ey voice: "It's okayyyy (insert baby nickname) . . . come give me a huggie."
4. Counting to three means so much more now.

Let's take a small break and please discuss point number three. Sure, I'll wait while you fill up your glass of wine or get another coffee. Why are baby nicknames for adults (and kids) so utterly disgustingly annoying? Well, at least I thought so until I had my own baby and began calling her a revolving combo of: little ballerina precious licious yummy pixie angel dust princess. The names were fluffy and long and never the same. Like a massive stick of cotton candy where you know it can't be good for you, but you just can't stop because it's so sticky and damn addictive.

Along with these changes comes a big metamorphic moment . . . whether it's while planning a dinner party, arguing with your husband, or suddenly pulling out your tweezer in the Zara changing room because the light is just simply perfect for plucking those fine hairs. We have all had those moments where you think *oh shit*. It's happened. Yup, it's official. I am turning into my mother. As if that were the most God-awful thing. It's not because the most awful thing will be when your daughter hates being compared to you.

Certain things in life are good for the soul. I'm not talking about vitamins and superfoods. What I'm talking about is much deeper. What I'm discussing is intangible. Things such as sisterhood, daughterhood, and the ultimate "hood" of all. Motherhood. Many have said that we have children because mothering is good for the soul. This is something I say embrace as a "sure of." Before actually becoming a mom, I read. I read everything. I read about why you need to exclusively breastfeed for the first six months of your child's life because that is the only way. I learned that if you put an infant on a semi torturous schedule, that you would be able to catch some sleep. I read that in some cultures the pregnant and post-pregnant body is considered beautiful and sacred but that I was not from one of those cultures. No, no, I was from the culture where trainers came to the hospital alongside a dietician to start the weight loss as soon as possible. There was an art to becoming "baby-wise!" and I was on a mission to master it.

My first day alone with Gnocchi? My mom had left. Mr. Excel was back at work. And I didn't have a fat Kenyan. I had a skinny woman from Burkina Faso. I know what you're thinking, "Of course that woman can find magic in mommyhood cause she isn't cleaning up the mess." And to this I will say she was more for me. I wanted to be the perfect mom and let's just say she let me do that and reminded me what my daughter's name was when I forgot. And then because I live in Dubai I quickly learned how to complain about my diamonds being too bright and my Porsche being too fast. Right after complaining about the lack of greenery and culture.

So, what did I do? I knew I was supposed to love and cherish this time and bond with Gnocchi, but I did neither. I quickly and rather selfishly realized that this was neither easy nor fun. It was scary being without my mom. Like someone was asking me to jump out of a plane alone. Without a parachute. Over concrete. I thought I would call some guru of sorts—someone who would make it sound simpler. I called my mom, she didn't answer, and I guess would've called my MIL but didn't trust the advice of a woman who stole butterflies from a butterfly garden. Is she normal? So that left . . .

Me: "Teta? I'm home now and all alone and now what? Gnocchi's looking at me like I should be doing something. I've changed her, spoken to her, and have even done a little Macarena dance. What now?"

Teta: "Rub warm olive oil all over her body, then put her pacifier in whiskey to ensure a good night's rest. Then cut her eyelashes, shave her head, and put bat's blood on her arms and legs to make sure she doesn't get hair there."

Me: "Umm . . . okay. More Macarena dancing it is!"

Bye, bye, free time. I want you to physically, emotionally, and spiritually wave good-bye to it. I mean this. Even if you're blessed enough to have a nanny/regular babysitter/your sister/mom/aunt/cousin or all of the above living down the street from you, even then. Now, stop slapping your forehead in question of how you got yourself into this. I know, I know, it sounds extreme, but I cannot overstate it. Every time I try to tell someone that the free time you once had before breeding "shrivels into nothingness" along with your placenta, they are almost certain I am lying or at the very least exaggerating. Let me be clear, it's not that there is literally no free time although that's exactly how it feels. No, it's more that any free time you have feels so precious and so endangered that you don't know what to with it. It's like a rare species and so critical to your survival that it is often lost on mundane tasks. You panic with the free time you have between pumping and breastfeeding and writing in her journal and folding her outfit for tomorrow. This endangered breed known as "free time"—or "you time" becomes a point of focus well into your first year of mommyhood. I'm actually not sure where the species lives or if they're even breeding at all anymore. Point is they are practically all poached by our husbands and children.

Breastfeeding goes wrong all the time, but people deny it. Yes, that seems to go against the laws of the natural world where peanut butter and jelly are meant to be united forever, and where *za'atar* and *labneh* make such a great marriage. Yes, breastfeeding is supposed to be magical but for a whopping percentage it is not. Don't get me wrong. If it works, and you have no problems doing it, it's great. If it works, it's the best thing on earth.

And so, where was I at, ranking wise? What was my scorecard? My scheduled C-section wasn't a "real delivery" according to my MIL. Yes, you read that right. Being cut open wasn't enough. The fact that I didn't find breastfeeding magical and oh-so-fulfilling was also terribly non-maternal of me according to my MIL. No, we get along great, why?

But know this: anyone who says the only way you can feel real love and bond with your baby is to deliver naturally where the nurse plops the baby on your chest (who immediately starts sucking) is a liar. Down to the core. Don't let anyone make you feel like your birth was a "C" and not an "A+."

Unless it's your MIL telling you that C-sections don't count.

Don't let anyone make you feel like your birth wasn't the best it could be. Nobody really plans on feeling disappointed about how it all went so just don't go down that road. Don't do that to yourself. This time it's not only social media that makes us feel like we are supposed to have a perfect everything. It's actually every older female in your life telling you that. A long list of *ya reits* (I wish) sprinkled with a bunch of should'ves and could'ves. But mostly it's our own expectations of birth, and *that* is much harder to unfollow and unlike.

The Why of the Cry

Whether or not you married a man who's willing to run red lights to get home in time to catch bath time or not, dads are outsourcers by nature. They are accustomed to working hard, yes, but also smart! I'm not even talking about whether or not they're willing to change a poopy diaper. Rather, I'm addressing the fact that some guys are under the misconception that poop doesn't even happen. Take fifteen seconds and reread that.

I'm assuming you, too, would be far from pleasant if you had just pooped your pants, were hot and sweaty, a little hungry and gassy, and yet instead of being changed, fed, and burped you were lugged around by a hairy ape who kept holding you up to his face saying "*jagal*" (translated: big man) and showing you off. It is of, course, all relative. I'm just saying there are dads that can zone out to the stares and cries and believe the false fact that "Babies cry. That's what they do," instead of investigating the why of the cry. Then, you have the other camp of fathers who strongly believe there is a huge reason behind every peep your little one makes.

My husband is of the latter camp. He's gotten much better though so we're not divorced . . . yet. But, whenever Gnocchi made the tinniest grunt, Mr. Excel was all over it, annoyingly asking me to explain the why of that cry. An existential moment. I'm not saying that I wasn't jumping at every tiny squeal and noise she made. I was—but I wasn't looking for an explanation. I was chalking it up to one of the following: hungry, gassy, poopy, sleepy, or bored of our faces. But, since Mr. Excel needed the big reasons behind each little gurgle, I pulled my "fake it until you make it" sleight of hand.

"Ohhhh she's trying to ask you what time you'll be home tonight." Obviously, it wasn't true—or was it? Or "Hmmm I don't think she likes the way your mom just spoke to me." Or "She doesn't like your tie." Whatever your husband's way may be, let him be him and try your best not to comment. Rolling your eyes is a silent comment by the way, so stop that, too.

First-Time Mama Math

I prefer words. I love them, actually. No right or wrong answer. No miscalculation or angle measured incorrectly. That pressure is off in writing because the length of your sentences is for you to define. Math is the complete opposite. It's all about rules and exceptions to that rule you *just* learned.

Number of times you check to see if baby breathing while sleeping: 5,672
Diapers changed in the last twenty-four hours: 29
Minutes spent trying to burp your little one: 56
Minutes spent trying to get baby to latch before switching boobs: 84
Messages to your sister saying you need a break: 17
Photos of your face you send to your mama each day: 11

Total: doesn't really matter because you're officially sleep deprived. But, wait, what kind of sleep-deprived mama are you? Wakey, wakey, it's quiz time! Note, I am keeping these short, as well as the sub-chapters in these chapters . . . because, well, your ability to follow a long *anything* has officially been quartered.

1. Upon waking, you:
   a) Chug that coffee from last night
   b) Pump and chug
   c) Pump

2. Last thing before you collapse for a few hours you:
   a) Have a sip of your husband's wine
   b) Pump and sip
   c) Pump

3. Rocking your screaming baby back to sleep at 4 a.m., your mantra is:
   a) Hakuna matata my ass
   b) Umm . . . tomorrow is gonna be better . . . it better be
   c) This too shall pass

Mostly As: You don't take things to heart and you only follow the rules after breaking a few of them along the way. Okay, more than a few. You believe in "happy mama, happy baby" despite how colicky your baby is.

Mostly Bs: You're in the zone. You knew it would be hard but you're playing the mama role you were born to portray. You may develop chronic fatigue syndrome in a few months but for now this is working!

Mostly Cs: You're a perfect mom. A mommy unicorn. That exists. It's you. Now, admit you lied about your responses to this quiz. It's okay. You can whisper it. Nobody's judging.

When your hibernation phase is almost over you may book an appointment to get your roots done and mentally prepare yourself for your big reveal. You are a mama now and choosing what color to paint your nails is more crucial than ever. Engine red to show that you're still fun and sexy? Or cloudy winter white to show a more maternal, mature side of you? Star rhinestones are always an option. I find myself reading headlines in order to say something at a dinner and drinks party other than, "Oh do you have kids?" Silence. If they did I would automatically fixate on a tiny thing and create a bond. "Oh my God that is so funny, I too love carrots and dip. What are the chances? This is a sign we really need to hang out. NO, really. Give me your number. Hmmm and how do you spell your name?" At this point I was losing my knack for making three new besties during every trip to the restroom. I can (COULD?) no longer remember people's names. You are unrecognizable. It's okay. C'mere. Ugly cry all you like.

15

COMPARISONITIS

(MATERNAL OLYMPICS)

I was grabbing lunch in DIFC, when I saw a tiny baby. I had already forgotten how small they are when they come out because Gnocchi was two months old at the time. I saw this tiny person—he couldn't have been more than a week old—dressed in a suit. No, not a onesie with the image of a suit printed on it (I still find those cute) I'm talking a real suit: Okay, it was too hot for the jacket but this kid was wearing pants, a tie, and a button-down shirt and was shrieking at the top of his lungs. People were staring. I was staring. Actually, there wasn't one person who *wasn't* staring. This little baby's mother was teary eyed, while the proud idiot father was parading baby with the scorching hot sun of Dubai hitting his face directly. The baby was beetroot red and hating on his parents. It really never is too early for therapy. A ridiculous outfit, aggravated new mama, and a proud dad who is oblivious to others' feelings. Yes, we can all see your sperm "done good." No need for *that* many high fives.

If sometimes it's the dads going overboard on showing off their handiwork, more commonly it's the mamas. They don't call it Daddy Wars, do they? Nope, it's the mamas. They go obsessive-compulsive competitive. It ain't pretty. What month, how tall, magnitude of poop—all gauges of whom their child is going to most resemble: the likes of Bill Gates, Steve Jobs, Venus Williams, or Céline Dion?

I blame the damn hormones (DH). I've come to blame *everything* on DH. Missed a flight? DH. Out of yogurt? DH for not remembering to write it on the list. Turned into a comparison-competitive-mama-milestone monster? DH and possibly a lack of coffee. Husband still annoying you? DH. Three kids and five years into momification, I still blame it on the hormones. And teething. What a mystery those two huge buckets are.

Oh, and by the way, those mommyhood forums with their stupid abbreviations for everything? DH is "dear husband" on there. But, to you and me, DH is DH. *wink*

Life wouldn't be as good without a little bit of volatility. You know . . . the ups and downs . . . breakdowns and breakthroughs. And the best moments in my opinion manage to capture both. Babies are born facilitators of these moments. It's a form of such accelerated love instilled to make you look after them and jump out of bed when they are crying for their pacifier or a diaper change. Or as they get older to ask you where angels live and if they can have a glass of water and then that they have to pee. The potential they have to solve the bulk of the world's problems is incredible yet goes untapped because the catch-22 is we just want them to go to sleep.

When You Fall in Love . . . with Corn Bits

And then you fall in love again. Why do I have to love the smell of her poo-poo? Would poo-poo by any other name smell as bad? It is particularly pleasant when it is halfway up her back and she is in need of a hose-down to get rid of the smell. However, you personally feel about poop—it is the high point of every mother's day. It is how we assess how our babies are doing. You know, on the inside. How many poops is indicative of whether or not they are getting enough nutrition—and when you're breastfeeding it also indicates what you ate yesterday. Color, consistency, clarity, and cut . . . just kidding, it is nothing like a diamond. Except it's as precious to you when they *don't* manage to make one for an entire day.

So, like most good things in life, it's a process. In the beginning I loved it, then I hated it right when she started eating solids because, well, it's poop and sometimes there'd be corn bits wedged in there. And yet, it was MY poop. A part of her that I felt responsible for and attached to.

Let me remind you, Mr. Excel is of Arab descent—just like me—and he too grew up in a bunch of different countries, mostly Western, but also like Saudi. So he's caught in the middle between Western and Arab. It is because of that he has a profound resistance to diaper changes. Remember that conversation in a bar after trying to change my nephew's poopy diaper and help the other one on the potty? When Mr. Excel suggested I handle all the poopy stuff? Well, it stuck.

I rarely left Mr. Excel alone with my daughter for fear of SSP (Stinky Smelly Poop). A very technical term, yes. But, one fine day, we agreed I'd join a casual coffee with friends, a little late—no more than fifteen minutes—and left our daughter with him. I was literally in the middle of my permissible fifteen minutes (which he claims was forty-five . . . and men say that women exaggerate?) when I got a frantic phone call. "SHE DID IT! SHE POOPED! WHERE ARE YOU? ARE YOU ALMOST HERE?"

Did I shake my head, a bemused smile on my lips, tell him to change her stinky butt, and continue with my coffee?

Heck no. This was code SSP and those monsters are mine, all mine.

I rushed out and cabbed it the five-hundred-meter distance he was from me, which probably took longer than it would have taken if I had walked, but, in the moment, I wasn't thinking straight. I had to get to the poop ASAP. When I finally got there, breathless, Mr. Excel was calmly sipping his Americano while Gnocchi *was nowhere to be seen*. He assured me (yes, that's meant ironically) that a mutual friend of ours was in the restroom with my baby.

Ummm, what? He outsourced it?

Logically, yes, I should have just accepted this and (according to her husband), "thanked them nonstop for not keeping my daughter in her poopy diaper," but that's not what happened. I was furious. Why couldn't her dad who was physically there, stopped drinking his damn Americano for a second to either hold her and keep the poop fumes from drifting over everyone, or change her himself? Absolutely ridiculous. Cue a whole scene and some nonverbal tension later (the worst kind, if you ask me), which was topped off with an awkward uncontrollable show of irrational emotions from my side. I decided to isolate the "takeaways" from this.

Several, albeit forced, thank-yous later, and a few minutes to think rationally about what had just gone down, I came to the same conclusion I started with. It is a conclusion that only moms will understand and agree with. Take a moment now because this will hit you hard. Moms have an official carte blanche (remember?) and can do or say anything they want when it comes to their kids. So, if I want to be the only one to change her poop then so be it, that's what's going to happen. I mean, I wasn't cut open to let someone else enjoy the SSP without some clearance from me. That's just the way it goes. Corn bits and all. Maybe I was mad I had missed it. Maybe I was disappointed that as I rushed into the bathroom in hopes of finding her lying on the changing table only I saw my reflection in the mirror and I was too late. I had become unrecognizable. A mom who was upset about someone else changing her daughter's poop. Unheard of—yet so common.

I suddenly knew that it was stupid to be devastated but I couldn't shake that feeling off. I was. And devastation looks ugly on me (but honestly, who rocks devastation?). I'd been robbed of analyzing the poop and then complaining about it to other moms. "And then she took the biggest poop in the French restaurant of all places and I had to spray air freshener after changing her!" Oh, well. I had no doubt that there would be other poops and surely other *magical* moments where I would be unrecognizable. I just had to be patient and wait for more . . . uh, magic.

Why Insta-Mommies Are a Hate/Love Thing

If you think you're a little bit type A . . . well, get pregnant, have a kid, and see how fast your competitiveness is redefined. Trust me, it goes higher. Way higher. You cannot help but compare yourself to other women during pregnancy. Embrace it though because there will always be someone who will have gained a total of nine pounds throughout her entire pregnancy and whose cravings consist of lettuce, water, and grilled chicken. You will also know someone who had contractions for twenty minutes, barely broke into a sweat, and popped the baby out within the hour. Now listen to me carefully, these people are one of two things—they are either not human or they are liars. The sooner you come to terms with the fact that one of these two situations are true, the sooner you can also start analyzing what type of mom you are and where you fall on the maternal Olympic scale of competiveness.

1. How do you document your baby's growth?
   a) By generally remembering her birthday—at least getting the month right.
   b) By having a photographer on standby to take a pic every day for the first year. And, yes, of course she will be wearing the same outfit and be in the same pose.
   c) At the pediatrician where her height, weight, and head size are measured.

2. What events do you celebrate in your baby's life?
   a) Graduation from college.
   b) *Every day* and you are fully committed to sending out a WhatsApp alert for every coo, burp, and poop that she makes.
   c) The big 0-1.

3. What do you do when your baby cries?
   a) Roll your eyes and close the door muttering "babies."
   b) Call the pediatrician and 911 and your husband who is out of town for work. Immediately Skype your mom and frantically shake things in her face while you debate if you should rush her to the ER.
   c) Check for poop, fever, temperature, or anything that may be stuck in her eye or nose. When you don't find anything, immediately start calling your baby high maintenance.

Mostly As: Ummm, you might wanna step up your game here.

Mostly Bs: You might wanna relax and find a friend who chose mostly As.

Mostly Cs: Keep doing what you're doing and help those As and Bs out a bit, will ya? Everyone will thank you for it.

Remember when I wrote during the pregnancy chapters that I felt everyone else's experience will seem bigger, faster . . . dare I say better than yours? When your baby is out this doesn't change. It only gets worse. In today's world we are all becoming rewired to show ourselves as the biggest, fastest. Put down your phone/Kindle/tablet for a sec and tell me I ain't lying. Tell me you don't want a whole marching band cued up for a live rendition of "Hallelujah."

Something not many mamas Insta-story about, though, is when your husband starts getting antsy and needy six weeks in. Your new addition to the family is finding a rhythm. Okay, not really, but he's trying to convince you that you are now totally handling this baby-stuff. Your reality is all pump, breastfeed, burp, change poop, and occasionally brush your teeth. It is a never-ending job that is so hard you question why you wanted it in the first place until she holds your pinkie again. And smiles from gas. You'll take it. Not before sobbing silently in the shower. And meanwhile, your beloved wants to get hot. But your leaky boobs and leaky eyes make reliving your honeymoon just a tad hard.

The last thing on your mind is your husband—his needs and wants. But, you know you have to be a supportive wife (do you? Says who? Teta?) and writing a bunch of thank yous and "my life will never be the same again because of you" in a card I handed over to Dr. Annie. But not before printing her a photo of *her* baby to give her (I love it when ob-gyns claim it's *their* baby after delivering them into the world—I guess they kinda are). I hugged her, sobbed a little into her shirt, and listened to her tell me to, "Go and have fun in your marriage again!" I love that she assumed I was counting down the days like an advent calendar. I was not, although I was eating a hell of a lot of chocolate.

As if that wasn't enough, my sacred good mornings and good nights are all f'ed up. I am a morning person by nature. I'm ready to bounce out of bed the moment the first rays of sunlight pierce through the tiny space left between our blinds. So, it's not like I used to be the type of woman who needed her cigarette, two coffees, and to check three social platforms before actually being physically able to say, "Good morning" (with a smile, God forbid). I'm more of a "Yay, the sun is up, there are things to be done, music to be heard, things to be said, dance moves to be performed." Don't hate me. It's genetic. Scientific studies have proven that 95.6 percent of who we are as people can be traced back to how we react to caffeine and hiccups.

Doesn't the 4.4 percent of that fake fact make it seem like it could be believably authentic? Truth is, I was raised in a house with parents who were the total opposite of one another. My mom? Not so much of a morning person. My dad? The definition of a morning person. His morning routine consists of: saying good morning a minimum of sixty-five times, Arabic newspapers, Nescafé, then endless jokes, laughs, and stories. This is all before 8 a.m. Difficult after a night of clubbing. Difficult even when you've had twelve hours of sleep, but his enthusiasm for the morning is somehow contagious and I seem to have caught the bug. Not to say my mom is unpleasant in the morning, on the contrary, she is just normal.

These mornings 4 a.m. means a sleepless night of rocking, swaying, and wiping burps up. With those fifty-six burpies I bought. At least the person being rocked, swayed, and wiped down was now a little part of me who weighed thirteen pounds. Helpless on a whole other level but so damn cute.

Babe-Onics

I have been transformed. Not only physically, mentally and emotionally, but also my mannerisms, priorities, thought processes, and yes, my voice. For some reason before I became a mom I didn't believe my friend when she told me, "Your body will be hijacked, and your mind will be held hostage." I now get it. I have days where I barely recognize myself, my voice, or my boobs. I wasn't prepared to not feel like myself. I wonder if I should ask the pharmacist to give me some Vitamin B_{12} to keep my nerves in check and my confidence, too, because I feel like crap. But, I don't think I can take his high-volume diagnosis from across five pharmacy aisles.

Along with this, I've had a major shift in my vocabulary. Long gone are my conversations about the latest outbreak of Ebola and Syria and where to donate or the concept of happiness and why Bhutan has it right. Instead they have been replaced with conversations about avocados, naptimes, what formula are you using, and the controversy that comes with using flashcards "duckkkk this is a duckkk what does the duck say?" Often times coupled with a life lesson: you should let criticism and any harsh words roll off you like water off a duck. There has been a shift in vocabulary, perspective, and wardrobe choices. Your intonation becomes squeaky, overly excitable, and erratic to say the least. You will quickly find the spark and newness in well, just about everything.

"Look baby, these are my socks! Socks were invented to keep our feet warm! Isn't that fun? Sometimes people wear them incorrectly and are true fashion faux pas. Socks should only be worn with running shoes and running shoes should only been worn in the gym. Bravo!" Burping achievement high fives quickly become a frequently used hand gesture. Don't judge. Pointing becomes so much more than pointing—should we get her the balloons when she points to them or is she just asking for a definition?

And why do they call them diaper bags when there are clearly about a thousand more things in there than diapers? Why on earth would I need a stapler, mustard, hair dryer, and toothpicks all in one bag? Who has ever needed the combination of those things? That is, with the exception of MacGyver. I loved MacGyver for making us feel like any combination of anything could be combined and soon enough, believe it or not, you could make mix that that extra lint at the bottom of your dryer at home with some pomegranate juice and of course an empty can of corn to create a fire engine.

Dear Gnocchi: I'm sorry for everything I didn't know. I didn't realize that that specific cry meant you were gassy because I had indulged in a lentil salad the night before and then proceeded to breastfeed you. I thought shampooing your hair, okay, bald head every night would help you sleep better—not that it would give you a bad cold at two months. I didn't mean to shove the pacifier in your mouth every time you cried, it was just something that sort of happened and you seemed to like it. My bad. You probably hated me when I decided it was too much dummy soothing time and that we had to cut you off cold turkey two months in. I'm sorry for recording every single cry, documenting every single arm movement and foot movement in utero and out. I experienced all these moments through the lens of a camera, but forgive me, it was all too exciting not to replay back for complete strangers. I'm really, really sorry for not being fluent in newborn. My bad.

Milestone This

Groundhog Day. It seems as though every new mom, no, let me rephrase that, every new type-A mom tries their best to get their "angel" into a routine. The second they're in that routine one of three things happens or maybe all three:

1. They grow out of the routine because, after all, you can't expect the same milestones to be met, same quantity of food to be fed, and same vaccination mental preparation to be experienced at various ages. One week in a baby's life can be equated to going from elementary to junior high: you are no longer in the same classroom for all of your classes. They actually expect you to walk down the hall to science class? The pressure.

2. You get a sudden "Groundhog Day" feeling come over you. Each day seems to be the same. Every. Single. Minute. This drives you mad and you break bubba out of their routine out of sheer boredom. The new bedtime is at 10 p.m. tonight. You will quickly learn why this is a total disaster and try and undo it at eight.

3. Someone has an opinion. The usual culprits, yes. NO surprise there. Both equally annoying at this stage and you often find your MIL and Teta equally annoying and giggling when talking about your philosophy on co-sleeping and routines.

So, you have that dreaded existential moment where you ask yourself, "What am I doing with my life?" You WhatsApp your mom to which she sends a barrage of irrelevant emoticons. Very helpful, mom.

Now, this completely depends on how involved you are as a mom, whether or not you hold down a full-time job or decided to start a business with a newborn, and how much of a schedule and control freak you are. I will say that I am a schedule freak. Yes, I'm spontaneous and carefree and fun-loving but there is definitely something to be said about having a schedule to follow! I know I said throw away your schedule back in Chapter 14. Don't hate me for my lack of a sustained party line.

So, you become milestone obsessive. Just roll with it. Month by month.

Month 1: You think to yourself, is this it? She's so precious with her cute little cry. Awe. So innocent and mouse-like. And she thinks she's scaring us? "Awwww hush now little one," and you proceed to shove a boob or pacifier in her mouth.

Month 2: Ohhhhh, okay, so the crying thing does get old fast.

Month 3: Is that a smile? Oh, wait . . . a poop. But, that's okay, we can smile while we poop. Multi-tasking.

Month 4: How much does tummy time annoy you? Ohhh, a lot. Okay, sorry.

Month 5: Solids? Two camps of kids here: yes please or ohhhhh (loud gag) not yet!

Month 6: Definite babbling and sitting. Kinda sitting up is both normal and extraordinary here. Okay, so sitting with a lot of support. Like you and fifteen pillows. You quit drinking liquids so as to not leave them for even a second for fear that that may topple over. Don't worry, I won't make the Leaning Tower of Pisa reference here. Too expected.

Month 7: Crawling anyone? Too fat to suddenly move? Well, then it's straight on to walking for you!

Month 8: Still in love with breastfeeding? Baby-led weaning? Both—you guessed it—normal.

Month 9: She don't know what sharing is yet, but she's holding on tightly to what it is that you want/love. Nine out of ten times it's your hair. Fast-forward six months and you find a bald spot.

Month 10: Say it with me. Separation anxiety to the hundredth degree. There should be a theme song for this stage: "Without You"?

Month 11: Almost one. She's getting vibes from you that you can't wait to potty train her because your face scrunches up at all her best poops.

Month 12: Happy birthday. She's thinking, "That candle looks yummy." You're thinking, "What a genius! Look at how intent her gaze is. Nobel Prize winner for sure."

Who are these experts who drew up the milestone lists anyway, and do they even have kids? Gina Ford, Ferber, Dr. Spock, Supernanny, the La Leche League. The websites and blogs you used to spent countless hours on are all replaced by www.babycenter.com. Everything becomes a fixation. When Gnocchi started sitting up she would lift her arm out and bend her elbow. I googled every variation of "preference to bend one arm" I could come up with and marched into every check-up at the pediatrician's armed with a list of questions. There are many different schools of thought when it comes to baby behavior. And many ways to avoid getting into arguments or mommy wars about which way is *best*. There is no best. There just isn't because every baby is different just like every uterus is unique. Yep. I'm still banging on that drum. And will be until you write it down. C'mon, get out your journal.

You will always meet some mom silently judging you and laughing into her sleeve about your baby in the pediatrician's waiting room— "Oh!" She'll say, "My baby was sleeping through the night at one month! She's currently potty training herself at nine months. How old's yours? Of course, it's bad that yours isn't! They're almost twelve months old!" To which I always want to reply, "But your baby just ate a box of tissues and some dirt, so . . . you know, we all have our battles to pick."

I have to admit, for the first year I would religiously read *What to Expect When You're Expecting* again and again and write down the specific milestones: Cooing? Check. Picking up object with one hand? Check. Passing the object from one hand to another? Check. Razzing, what the? What the hell is razzing? Oh, it's a wet sound? Why is that even desired as a developmental step? I really think that all of the baby lingo is put in place for no other reason than to stress out and ostracize first-time moms (FTMs) from veterans.

Oh, and the shopping from your buymester just continues. Get used to that. When in doubt you will buy 26,398 items you believe will be your magic pill, your silver bullet to fix the current issue.

I had absolutely no justification for buying So. Many. Pacifiers. No, really. But my take? Happy wife with hands full of bags? Happy life. The key to keeping your husband happy about how much over-spending you do is to buy a few "I love my daddy" and "Daddy's girl" bibs.

16

THE WHEELS ON THE BUS

(iF YOU'RE HAPPY AND YOU KNOW iT)

It's about this time—three or five months of age—that you feel like you're supposed to be educating them. Tummy time is boring for everyone. You need a bit of socializing, so you sign up for a mama and baby class. Like, say, a music class. You're optimistic. Here's exactly what goes through your mind though during the entire one-hour class:

1. I'm beginning to think they have a "no shoe" policy to see who has the most unkempt toes.
2. Why have only five minutes gone by?
3. These are precious moments that will be gone before I know it. Forty-three minutes left.
4. I really hope she appreciates this, I mean there's really lots of better things I could be doing with my time.
5. I wonder if having my toenails pulled off would be less painful or an equal form of torture.
6. I didn't sign up for this. I mean, I did . . . my name is on the registration, but I didn't really "sign up for this" if you know what I mean.
7. How bad would it be if I brought my mini iPad next week, or better yet, sent her alone?
8. Note to self: make sure your iPhone is fully charged before the next class. Who said you can't sing and shop?
9. Is that clock working?
10. Would the other moms judge me if I brought in a flask?

11. Our generation is absolutely ridiculous about these classes . . . did our parents endure this torture?
12. For the price of these classes, I could have totally paid for a weekend escape in an Airbnb.

You can send me the $145 I just saved you via PayPal. You're welcome. Okay, so maybe it wasn't so bad. After all, I do have six whole days to recover before the next class. Ugh. Sing it with me: "*If you're anxious and you know it clap your hands!*"

The Soundtrack to the First Year

Magicians use this term to try and explain how smooth they are in accomplishing and completing a trick: *sleight of hand*. Did I have it? Maybe, just maybe, it has something to do about managing to pee with a three-month-old who's still hanging from your Baby Bjorn. Or maybe, just maybe, sleight of hand is the resistance and control you call on to stop sarcastically face-palming when your husband moans he has a sore back from a fifteen-minute Baby Bjorn session.

Our house is forever filled with the cacophony of children's songs, obnoxious farm noises, and dogs howling. All from baby toys. Investing in a decent set of earplugs is sounding better and better every day. And just like that not only do your conversations, body, and rate at which you lose your hair change, but so too do the sounds and smells and sights of your home. Not that they would save me from myself, mind you . . . I currently have an obsession with turning everything into a catchy tune. I also constantly scratch and sniff the discolorations on my clothes in this new game I invented: What's That Stain?

So, I sing. No, like a lot. Brushing my teeth is a performance worthy of an *American Idol* finale and you should hear my diaper changing rap—there are multiple verses and sometimes my husband chimes in with an R & B beatbox bit if he's home from work early enough. Rather than roll his eyes or wince, he joins in as back-up singer, or on air-guitar—eyes shut, face-scrunched, and everything. That's how I know I married the right guy.

I'd like to think she knows we're in this thing together, even when I do the crazy chicken dance or sing stupid songs about tying my shoes. I've actually started making notes on what you need for a successful music class. I'm still not really sure if these classes are for the kids or the moms. A part of me strongly feels like it's just a get-away for moms to take their screaming babies to scream alongside other babies. Why so many of the songs have the annoyingly overly British, nautical word "Ahoy" I have yet to understand.

We've all complained about one of these classes and endured the singing, mouthed along, and plastered on a fake enthusiastic grin when our little ones glance over at us to see if we, too, are having as much fun as them. That same smile is plastered on when my little one turns to see if I, too, also find Ollie the owl to be absolutely hilarious when he thinks he's lost his tail. Shoot me. And then she pooped and I was busy changing her and thinking what would be so hard in teaching them the lyrics to Biggie Smalls? Totally doable and I bet you the classes would be filled with much less eye rolling.

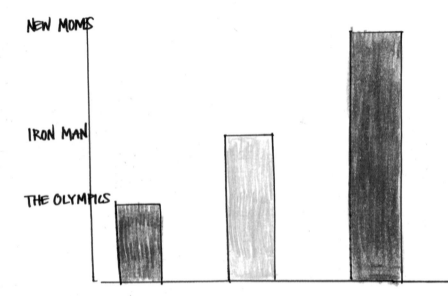

NEW MOMS

IRON MAN

THE OLYMPICS

LEVEL OF COMPETITIVENESS

CRAWLING TO FIRST BIRTHDAY

You think you're tired but you have no idea. You think you know, but you don't. Your baby's almost one and that means next year she'll be two and the year after that, three . . . and, well, you know the rest. There are all these new pressures and shit I really don't know like the fact that fish don't cough. They don't, by the way, and other random facts that I'm *obliged* (okay, call it obliged or call out the overachiever in me who does it because she loves it) to put on Post-its and stick on her snack box. As if it wasn't stressful enough without what I can only describe as the *Jeopardy!*-esque pressures. She's in kindergarten now. But until you get to that stage you become toe obsessed, finger obsessed, and obsessed with taking photos and videos and using Snapchat filters and sending it to . . . EVERYONE . . . until they ask you to stop. Or block you. Baby milestones and purées are what your months are jam-packed with now, though, and you share like everyone's up all night wondering if she preferred carrots or apples. And just like that your baby's one and you have less time than ever before.

That is, until you get pregnant again.

17

ABRACADABRA

(THE MAGIC YOU DON'T WANT)

Like any child, I was convinced (and still am) that I am my mom's favorite. When I would ask her just to be sure, she used to roll her eyes and say, "Who's my favorite? Hmm . . . the one who's sick until he gets better, the one that's tired until he is rested, and the one who is injured until he is healed." A little melodramatic, but, yeah, makes sense. I think I then asked her but what if we were *all* rested, injury-free, and in good health with no runny noses . . . *then* who would your favorite be? She leaned over and whispered, "It's always been you. Always. In fact, I can't stand your brother and sister." Okay, fine, so I may have embellished that a bit. Okay . . . I totally made it up. But I get it now because there is nothing comparable to the heartache, pain, and worry of a mother when things go wrong. So the kid who is most in need of that mama lovin' in that moment is their favorite. Fair play.

Let's talk about the magic for a minute. I thought it all would be magical. I really expected there would constantly be soft music playing in the background while I rocked my baby to sleep for a total of nine seconds before heading out on date night with my husband because . . . well, why not? It *was* a Wednesday after all. I really thought baby puke wouldn't smell as rancid as it does, and I thought I would wake up every single day with a plan and that plan would actually be implemented play by play.

First, throw your schedule away. Just. Throw. It. Away. No one tells you this beforehand, but parenting is messy. And you will doubt yourself at every milestone. And every second of the day. Throw away your expectations and high hopes, too. You will look at other moms and think *What is their secret? What are they doing that I am not?*

And then there was this brace that I had to deal with. A stupid ugly brace. As if teething wasn't enough.

What brace? Let me turn this mommyfesto into a tiny sobfest for a minute. I want to unpack the fact that—and nobody ever warns you about this—sometimes you find yourself facing a tough, unfair situation. Like a medical situation. Or you lose someone close when baby's little and it colors everything. Or you realized you're massively postnatal depressed. There are so many things that can—and do—happen. I honestly believe every mama has a hiccup. Some shitty thing that is hard to bounce back from. I'll share mine, but I really want you mamas to share yours. Write to me about yours. I've been sharing these on *Huffington Post*. I truly do want to hear from you.

Okay, deep breath. Because writing about this is still a bit of a trigger for me. Here's what happened when Gnocchi was five-and-a-half months old.

Developmental dysplasia (or dislocation) of the hip (DDH) is an abnormal development of the hip joint. Gnocchi had it. She was diagnosed with that abnormality. The word "diagnosed" automatically makes it sound like a disease. Okay, let's not use that word. Umm . . . her condition was detected at five-and-a-half months. If you are a doctor you will probably be thinking, "Kinda weird that someone would wait so long to get an ultrasound or Xray when there were many red flags—born breeched, female, etc." And if you're not thinking that, then you're a) not a doctor or b) missed it like five doctors did. (Five doctors I am still mad at.)

Leonard Cohen famously wrote, "There is a crack in everything—that's how the light gets in." That resonated with me. It made sense. I barely knew what I was doing, and I had this crack. Fixable? Yes, but heartbreaking nonetheless. I suddenly wished my worries and stress boiled down to mere milestones. I wanted my situation to be ordinary, average, and a bit vanilla. Words I despised my entire life suddenly were these glittery magical signifiers I badly wanted back in my life.

In utero, since Gnocchi didn't turn around for so long she developed hip dysplasia. We are hoping that this will be a contributing factor to an Olympic/ballet career, where she will thank us for this and mention it in all her media interviews.

The day she was diagnosed, I suddenly had to mutely watch as the top pediatric orthopedic doctor put my baby into this strappy-looking cloth brace to keep her legs in a frog-like position. Dr. Marc Sinclair was tall and seemed to cower over her as he strapped her in. Despite the harsh reality of what he was doing, his touch was gentle and almost casual, as he had done this thousands of times before. He had, but it was a first time for us.

I was no longer present. I swear I immediately lost all five of my senses. In fact, the only thing I clearly remember was that I couldn't help hold her down as the doctor put the brace on her. As he explained how to put her in this contraption and where to put what strap and boot, all I could do was stand far away. My logic was that the further I was physically away from the examination table, the less likely this was really happening.

The Pavlik Harness—well, at least it had a cool name—was all white and a lot of Velcro. It looked like a body cast. And it made that peeling away sound Velcro straps make because they're all about never letting go. I remembered owning a pair of sandals I tried to fit my overgrown feet into for as long as I could. They were my favorite beach sandals and until now the sound of Velcro had reminded me of them. Now, I had a new, horribly scary association with that sound. I hated it and it had nothing to do with childhood sun-kissed memories.

Yes, it was scary. It changed her hips yes, but it probably changed me more. Sometimes you have to learn how to squeeze past something and go ahead and get those scratches that teach you how to get through things in the future. We absorbed medical terms and swallowed down protocols: "She can only be out of it one hour a day for her bath," and, "It's good news—she won't need surgery." As if that good news erased the painful new reality and we could breathe a sigh of relief. There were no high fives being given out here. As you can imagine, I googled . . . umm, everything? Pictures, videos, case studies, stories, fashion trends she could still sport when in this harness, obstacles she would be facing, and so on. The Pavlik Harness is designed to gently position your baby's hips so they are aligned in the joint to help normal growth and development of the hip joint. I read and reread that line. So final, so cold, so unemotional. The total opposite of everything I was and stood for.

Dealing with it was hard enough, but telling people was torture. It underlined the line I was dreading to mutter. It wrote it in red ink and drew a few arrows to point it out.

"She has hip dysplasia."

"Wait, what is it? How did she catch it?"

Because, after all, everything in the Middle East is caught, contagious, and can be fixed with a couple of Tylenol.

Why did I not see this pothole? Okay, so that's a totally bad analogy, but you get what I mean, right? Disbelief, shock, guilt, adaption, hope, positivity, and lingering fury. Some problems are not fixable, and I get that now, but it took me a while to feel blessed that this was. I was miles away from feeling like *saratonins,* my skype name and short-lived nickname my brother Karim had given me. It's kind of a version of serotonin, I guess. Serotonin is the happy hormone so not only was I depleted of that hormone, enzyme, chemical property, or whatever, but I didn't want to log into my Skype account at all so I made Mr. Excel Skype with his bestie from elementary school in Saudi Arabia who was now living in Sweden and happened to be an orthopedic surgeon so we asked away. Well, he did. I sobbed silently in another room.

It is not so much my difficulty to accept the condition as much as my difficulty to simply accept. I was being Velcro here. Unwilling to let go and go with the brace. No wonder I had right knee pain according to Louise Hay. I clung onto the fact that she was misdiagnosed, or rather, not diagnosed at all. I blamed myself. I blamed the five doctors who had missed it. Accepting this was my challenge. She was going to be wearing this for six to nine months and I had to somehow be okay with it. But I wasn't coping well.

Like all mamas, I wished it could have been me. I would have easily worn the brace for a year or ten if that meant that she didn't have to. She wouldn't learn how to crawl, stand or walk "on time." I couldn't put her in those short flirty dresses, cute jeggings, and baby Converse all parents who have girls look forward to. I struggled to hide the brace. Struggled to accept it. Struggled to protect her ego and mine from unnecessary stares, questions, and judgment. I struggled to shelter those fresh baby fat rolls from the pinch of the straps, which were leaving violent red marks where the skin, Velcro, and cloth all hugged too tight. This was a full-on parenting fail.

I was scared she would never crawl or walk and mostly that I wouldn't be able to love this child unconditionally. Could I hold her and fearlessly and confidently tell her everything was going to be okay? Wasn't that my job as a mom, though?

My fear was that she would catch on to me, read the look on my face, and see my less than enthusiastic and proud eyes. I was scared that she would somehow understand my non-verbals: "This is the hardest thing ever," and my anger that pushed aside the fact that this was what it was and focused on, "This is all that stupid doctor's fault." She'd read my fear and the disconnect this brace brought out in me. And here's where I can tell you from my heart to yours that I know for a fact that everyone's pothole is also internal. Everyone has a hiccup. Everyone hits their fair share of bumps in the road and has a crack in their otherwise seemingly perfect hand of cards. It's how you accept and adjust. My actual hiccup was clinging to ideas of perfection and how I imagined it *should* and *would* be. Everyone has their hand, their dose, and their story.

We all (hopefully) adapt and adjust, and if you're like me, the light that shines through the cracks is likely to be over-shopping. Yes, I adjusted with my credit card. And some soul searching, and a lot of tears. We made it through with the help of dresses and skirts (yes, to hide the harness, but also because, damn it, we both deserved some beautiful dresses at that stage).

Lucky Girl!

Mr. Excel's reaction to Gnocchi's hip dysplasia was that, if this is what we got, he'd take it. Like I said, I married a logical guy. And I'm not saying that as a throwaway line. I say that after really, really, *really* taking a minute to think about it. He's the epitome of logical. He's fair and just and understanding, but, well, most of all he has more common sense in his pinkie toe than I have in my entire body. This has played in my favor at times, but it's also part of what can make us argue. I mean sometimes a girl just gets super sad about socks, okay? No reason. He said, life is fair, and I had to agree.

So, let's revisit that rainbow-colored list of unicorn defecation . . . those mom-to-be promises I made back in Chapter 2 to myself, my husband, and my unborn kids. I had to reassess those. They went like this:

1. I will cherish every single day of pregnancy and not use bad language.
2. I will always make all of my kids' Halloween costumes every year.
3. I will wake up and go to bed with a smile on my face because happy mama = happy baby.
4. I will never fight with my husband around my baby (unborn or born). I will speak to him in a civilized and respectful manner at all times.
5. I will not be caught dead in track pants unless I am going to or coming from the gym.
6. I will always smell nice and have my hair and nails perfectly done to keep the romance alive in my marriage.
7. Organic, baby.
8. I will only listen to music that will heighten the possibility of my baby going to Harvard. Sorry, Kanye.

I took those eight promises and didn't reread them. I didn't bother rewriting them, either. I just did the easiest thing possible, which was throw them away. But you know, I've always relied on words—it's my go-to defense mechanism.

Those seven months, though, I don't know how I got through it, apart from the retail therapy. In the soul-searching part, I questioned if this was all because she is one-quarter Palestinian and hence had the stubbornness and need to do things her way.

My daddy (that dose of Palestinian in my genes) happened to visit us in Dubai when Gnocchi had been in that brace a few weeks and he assured us that we were lucky. "I *wish* I had been in a brace when I was a baby. Lucky girl." As a self-made man who walked from north Palestine to south Lebanon, my daddy wasn't one to dramatize or have a "woe is me and you" moment, even if it was warranted or well-deserved. I wasn't sure if he always tried to flip every problem on its head to show me how it was really an opportunity, or if he was just trying to get me to laugh. It sat well with me, though. It stuck.

And Teta? What did she have to say about the brace? "*Oo iza*," which roughly translates to "So what." Powerful stuff from this mama of nine. A widow at forty, she knew a thing or two about problems. This wasn't one in her books. She wasn't fazed at all. She didn't understand why I would be crying about having to strap my daughter in this Velcro trap of a harness for twenty-three hours out of the day. However, having a girl (and not a boy), now *that* was worth crying over.

Hindsight is twenty-twenty and I now know I could've handled Gnocchi's harness with more elegance. Now, I compare. I compare the level of freaking out to how much I am showing love. And I try to make the love come out on top. I know that sounds completely wrong. But you know what I mean. I am now able to love shamelessly, in public and behind closed doors. I can't help but question if maybe, just maybe, with Gnocchi's harness I did not give enough kisses and did a little too much covering up. I wish I had shown her that I was okay with it. She taught me how to start doing that, though.

Now, over almost four years later I still have hiccups. These days I face the possibility of breath holding syndrome and PFAPA, a periodic fever syndrome and autoimmune disease. There's always panic, but the type of panic that you can tame. I now grab that panic by the ears and don't let it set me off like hip dysplasia did. The cracks don't really stop happening. But as mamas we start to be more resilient to them, "Oh, another crack? *Oo iza* to you, Crack."

As adults we forget how to "roll with the punches." To be resilient, look at a challenge straight in the eye, and get our game face on to win over adversity. Babies and kids roll with everything. They dig rolling so much they'll try it on a changing table two-feet off the floor. Gnocchi was a constant reminder of all of those things. While I spent a lot of my days overexplaining her hip dysplasia, getting defensive, and overselling what she could do, Gnocchi was rolling over and spitting out lemon like all babies do. (Yes, the overselling was almost cute of me. When she was seven months old I'd claim she was not only babbling but forming complete sentences including vocabulary such as "globalization.")

Her perseverance prevailed. She still sat up on her own. She still gave us that charming, picture-worthy, sour face all parents wait for when she tried the lemon. She crawled and laughed and spat out broccoli purée. She made the hard bits easy and smoothed over our hesitations and our fears in dealing with her in this brace. She was resilient and obviously not taken aback in the slightest by her physical restriction and what I'm sure she saw as a temporary challenge.

I am now all about finding the light in the mess. In any mess. So, it's less of a mess and more of an opportunity. Thanks for the most useful brainwashing, Daddy and Leonard Cohen.

I have to say, I did a total sleight of hand abracadabra-style with that Pavlik Harness . . . and that's where even Teta saw the beauty of having a girl because, dresses and skirts. All. The Way. This was magic in action.

I do utterly love magic. I find it absolutely incredible that things can get hidden only to be revealed again after a few gestures and shakes. Much like life, I know. See how I made you think about that? Did you like how I equated magic and life? No? I know . . . nothing new, really, but still, kinda worth underlining again. No?

Sometimes you make these connections out of the cracks. I know that sounds wrong, too. But go with me here. Every so often you make a new friend who is a breath of fresh air and a real game changer. Aunty J (what my kids and husband . . . yea, awkward . . . insist on calling her) made the best chocolate chip cookies ever. With marshmallows. She was my neighbor who has a son a few months older than Gnocchi and forced me to laugh about the irony of my situation. She believed in sparkle the way that I believe in magic— that it was invented to make everything so much better. Like the fact that my teeth were in adult braces (orthodontics) for the same seven months that my daughter was in Velcro. Call it fate or call it the best lesson in patience—it was what it was—the reality of it. Everything difficult is an emotional mess of turmoil that we get consumed by, but if you focus on the facts then it's a totally different story. By focusing on the facts, you know with statements that can be proven with evidence and less feeling, well . . . then it's somehow much more manageable. Or so she tried teaching me, which took me a while to learn because sometimes I'm a slow learner. It actually took until I had my third child and realizing that he had breath holding (when a child cries so much that they hold their breath and faint) like my second. Fact. I also learned to dwell less, move on quicker, and accept that pastel pink really wasn't my color.

She told me, "Cry all you want but when you're done and you're ready to hang out and talk about something *other than* your daughter's hip dysplasia and how the many incompetent doctors in Dubai missed it, call me." Aunty J was right. Tough love resonated well with me and before we knew it we were suffering through those baby and mommy music classes together and giggling about songs called "Sand in My Sandwich" and any that had the word "Ahoy" in them.

She looked like what you would expect the perfect Westerner to look like (without making any generalizations here). She was blonde, blue-eyed, and chatty with a dry sense of humor whose jokes often made my coffee fly out of my mouth without hesitation. Her dress code on weekends was effortless, as in she didn't care enough to wear a bra on most days. She did what most of us wished we were comfortable doing. The daughter of a top ballet teacher in Baltimore and a psychiatrist, she was constantly twirling and plié-ing her way around corners and I was always impressed how she could dance and speak her way out of every problem. This was the same girl who couldn't get herself to stop using the f-bomb and refused to be "that mom" who used words like "fiddlesticks" to mask her anger.

We sang our way through tantrums rewriting the lyrics to more than a few musicals:

> I feel tired, oh, so tired
> It's scary how tired I feel
> And so stressed out
> That my husband doesn't understand my pout.
> (Thank you, "I Feel Pretty," *West Side Story*)

> Where is a bed for me right now?
> A place I can lay my head to sleep
> I'm really so sick of my kids and want them to close their eyes
> without a peep.
> (Thank you, "Castle on a Cloud," *Les Misérables*)

Rhyming dance moves and being on key were subject to how caffeinated we were that day. Oh, and at this point I received an email stating I was being made redundant at work. Sayonara, cubicle. Our department was closing. Because why wouldn't it be? When it rains, it pours. When one door closes, another one opens. One bird in the hand are worth two in the bush. Okay, so the last proverb was a bit irrelevant but you get what sorts of things were going through my mind. And, anyway, wasn't I over that office job? Yeah. Losing my job (while still on maternity leave, might I add . . . yeah, it was a Dear Diary moment to say the least) led me to write this book. And doubt every single skill that I had. And force me to be okay with the unknown, question my qualifications, my resume, and what my purpose was. All good stuff. At least that's what Aunty J says.

Finding Your Bitcoin, Your "Currency"

Every mama has a currency. Hey, it's not lame, it's a superpower to call on. Our own personal Bitcoin. Everyone, according to the Japanese, has an *ikigai*, or "reason for being." Everyone. Take a minute and think about it. Finding it requires deep and often lengthy search of self, a lot of crying, and nonstop doodles with optional ramblings in a Moleskine notebook. I challenge you to find yours. It *can* be found.

For a while I strongly believed that my calling was something to do with reporting any event—large or small—birthdays, the 2006 war in Lebanon, or a simple sensational sunset. Being that journalist who captures the fairy godmother's secrets. I have been known to grab any object and use it as a mic and indulge in a "reporting live" spiel. I've kinda grown up since then (not really) and interpret *ikigai* to be similar to my understanding of "your currency"—it's your secret sauce and every mama has a bottle of it. It's what gets you, me, and Meryl Streep and Jennifer Lawrence going through the day, week, and year. (Yeah, I just put us in the same sentence as Jen and Meryl.)

Mama or not, it's what keeps you ticking. You think you know how and when it will manifest, but you won't. Will you be immune to the stickiest smell of Thai curry-infused poop or the most patient during tantrums about socks? No one *knows*.

I remember being in the park where kids naturally congregate just because there are less rules. I walked over to greet a friend and along the way had to stop and give the whole description of what Gnocchi was wearing. What the harness was. How I felt. If she was okay and about a thousand other questions. It was at this point I had actually considered printing out leaflets to pass out to save myself some time in answering, "No, her legs are not broken, it is not contagious, and no, I am not okay with it." And the unanswered questions that they thought but dared not ask, "Did that mama drop her baby and make up some weird sounding disease to cover it up?" No, that would've been rude. They were under the presumption that their lingering looks were much less hurtful. They were wrong.

But you see what I was doing right there was using my *ikigai*—which is humor. Using humor (mixed with a lot of worry) to propel me forward through every situation. You will have *your* currency. A language and payment method and vehicle to get you through it.

Snuggle in for another self-quiz, mamas! This one's to help you see which general bucket of *ikigai* you're packing. Your *ikigai* may be like mine—which is that of Mother Teresa's because that's how I roll. Not really. I just realized my zipper has been open for at least an hour so I'm the farthest thing from put together.

1. When your kids cry and throw a fit you:
    a) Roll your eyes and scream back, "What is the big f-ing deal about pressing the elevator button?"
    b) Immediately start hugging and rocking them despite a few kicks to the face because Love. Always. Wins. You'll get your bruised eye looked at later.
    c) Step back and analyze the situation before reacting. Breathe deeply and e-nun-ci-ate their w-o-r-d-s. You are cool, calm, and collected. You also do a lot of yoga. And maybe drink a couple too many glasses of wine at night.
    d) Perform a quick exorcism to scoot away the bad spirits that have taken over your two-year-old. You typically spend a lot of time in the woods to burn smudging wands of wild sage—leading you to invest in eyelash extensions from all the candles you've lit to "cleanse" your loved ones.

2. When they won't eat anything remotely healthy and are demanding Cheerios and ice cream for the fifth consecutive dinner you:
   a) Say, "No way, honey. Go to bed hungry."
   b) Prepare yet another bowl of Cheerios and add chocolate milk to ensure that they still love you and are happy because that's what *really* matters. Add E-number-laden sprinkles generously.
   c) Sit them down for a quick chat about nutrition and show them what a palm-size serving of protein looks like and what half a plate of vegetables means as you dish up quinoa and vegan sausages with a raw medley of kale. Yum.
   d) Fashion that extra sage into another smudging wand and see answer from question 1.

3. Something major happens. Let's not go into scary details, mamas, but everyone has their darkest fears. Say one even *almost* happens. You:
   a) Power through it with denial, anxiety meds, flying your mom in to help, and googling until your fingertips bleed. Get twenty opinions and scream into a pillow or into your husband's face. Externalize the pain.
   b) Dig deep to creatively visualize it all resolving within minutes or possibly hours. See the pain as a big fluffy cloud of pink cotton candy to float on. Make zero sense when you talk to anyone.
   c) Get fifty books and read as much as you can in one night. Take notes and drill holes in the wall to mount twenty whiteboards filled with scenarios. Embrace your role as the informed mama who will beat this thing to death (with a whiteboard, if necessary).
   d) See answer from question 1.

Mostly As: You are Mama Tyson. Maybe tone down the volume there, but at least you are dishing it straight and your kids will realize that life isn't always easy or handed to them on a platter. Tough love is your middle name.

Mostly Bs: You are Mother Teresa. Literally. You're all about keeping the peace, even if that means skipping work to hug it out and helping them achieve a mouthful of cavities and a case of scurvy.

Mostly Cs: You are Mommy Logic. You don't get it. There has to be a solution and you are going to be the one to figure it out. You've done all the reading, so you don't see why you can't take a bit from each of the greats (Gina Ford, Ferber, Supernanny) and mix them together to be right. All. The. Time.

Mostly Ds: You are Mom of the Eternal Belief Systems with a hint of Maman Voodoo. There's no judgment here, but take it easy on the spells and potions.

I'm somewhere between a C and D and I'm okay with letting sorcery prevail over logic on most days because I know Mr. Excel has it under control. Of course, these four archetypes don't encompass the whole kaleidoscope of moms out there, but it helps to categorize them. Whatever bucket you fall into, though, do not panic because you will eventually have to leave your child with a pair of foreign arms—a grandmother, or nanny, or daycare peeps—who will answer this quiz differently. Their influences will vary and soon enough you can blame someone other than yourself for her latest bad habit. What a relief. Right? But what matters is that there's no judgment here. It's your superpower. Your *ikigai* and no one else's unless they're a C like you.

18

ENTER FOREIGN ARMS

(A DIFFERENT KIND OF VELCRO)

It can take a lot to raise a baby. Not shocking news, no, but it can take a whole lot. A team, really. And with this team comes all sorts of different people and elements. These external factors have opinions and mannerisms that will annoy the shit out of you when it comes to you and your little one. It just will and that's okay.

It's really hard to fail in motherhood. Failing is pretty much when you forget your kids' name. Or when you're six hours late picking him up from the nursery, or when you lose your shit and yell instead of counting to that infamous 1-2-3 or feed them anything non-organic. Umm, did I mention how it's okay to fail?

But, let's not forget here that your main objective as a parent is to tire them out. I was wasting a lot of precious time with morning kisses and cuddles when I should have been in hyper, let's-run-around mode and a bit more of "What the hell, of course you can jump from the couch to the chandelier. Can you do it with your brother hanging from your ankles? Let's try, shall we?" Note to self: always have cushions on the floor for them to land on. Well, it wasn't so much "run around" per se for Gnocchi in her harness because her rendition of that was a few reps of "sit up," "sit down" followed by an hour or two of "peekaboo."

At some stage you are going to need to pass your baby into a stranger's arms—whether that's to grandparents so they can bond and you can get a break, or to a babysitter so you can finally get your hair done, or to your husband when you have something else going on, or to someone whose job is solely to help you when you need to help yourself first.

The morning Gnocchi started nursery I was traumatized. It was only a structured play place she'd be hanging out in a few hours each morning, but I think it permanently damaged me. The focus during these "adaptation" periods is always on the "bahbey" And, to this I say, no, not "poor bahbey." We should be saying "poor mohmmy."

Now, take a second to think about this before jumping on me with counterarguments like, "They're so little . . . and their emotions haven't yet developed." Or "They can't walk or talk yet to express their trauma." Or, "Separation anxiety *is a thing*!" Blah blah blah. Minor details. Us mamas are the ones with our hearts being broken when our child sobs as a complete stranger shoves a Sophie the Giraffe in her face. You want to shout, "WAIT, NO! She prefers elephants not giraffes actually and her eyesight is pretty good so no need to put it two centimeters from her eyeballs," but you don't. Instead you listen to the stranger's orders.

"Stand back . . . don't make eye contact. Tell her bye . . . smile as she sobs and reaches out for you. Walk out confidently." Suuuuuure. I turn just to give a fake cheerful and overly perky wave and in a shaky voice tell her to "have fun" only it sounds more like "ave un" because I can barely swallow let alone speak before I am immediately ushered into a brutal waiting room with other sobbing moms.

When you face this situation, you need to do the following steps repeatedly:

1. Acknowledge it sucks.
2. Cry in the shower.
3. Google things at all hours of the night and wear waterproof mascara and tons of blush to make yourself look perky and well put together.
4. Make friends with the owner of the nursery and convince her to install a CCTV camera to track your child. Have a backup tracking device implanted somewhere on little one in case CCTV fails you.
5. Make friends with a fellow mom so that you can sob and braid each other's hair in the waiting area. This will make the time pass more quickly as you ask each other dull questions that neither of you will hear the answers to while trying to stay busy and not focus on isolating your child's cry from all

the white noise in nursery. Six months later you will realize that her name is in fact Maya and not Julia, and she will realize you are a writer and not a lawyer.

6. Keep murmuring, "It's just a phase, it's just a phase." This works best when curled up in the fetal position at the back of the room. Rocking is optional. This is, after all, the go-to tactic in motherhood that never fails.

7. Bring snacks, a warm blanket, and a favorite toy . . . these things are for you.

8. Realize that nursery is only one step of many, and that you have a lifetime of "I hate yous" and "I love him . . . I'm gonna marry him anyway" and "I want to study interpretive dance and acting" to look forward to. Enjoy having the ability to scoop her off the floor and hand her a cookie to distract her while you can. Those years are numbered.

9. Realize everything in motherhood is just a phase and that, one day, she will have her own kids and criticize you for not knowing what you're talking about. Be sure to have hard copy proof of things you have done for her, including explosive poopy diaper changes.

10. Think of it as boot camp . . . mostly for you. And for your heart. It will hurt but it will make you stronger. Apparently. Also, I still don't see what's so bad in being a softie who sobs whenever a Johnson & Johnson baby shampoo commercial comes on. The music gets me every time.

11. Remind yourself of the bigger picture. This is another useful tip to carry with you throughout parenthood. Having issues potty training? I don't know of any child who goes to university in diapers. Two-year-old tantrums? There are anger management classes for adults who still have those. Don't you feel better? It just sucks *right now*. Not forever.

12. Have that one logical friend (probably from Eastern Europe) or older relative on speed dial. She will slap the tears off your face and remind you that you are lucky to be able to afford nursery and make fun of your unattractive ugly-crying face.

Every seemingly unbearable phase you get stuck in will eventually shift. Next week? Toddler tantrums. Repeat: "This too shall pass" with a little prayer, practice patience, and knock back a few shots of vodka. Ummm, possibly? But also, why not?

Family Feud

Now, let's talk about when it's your family—or his family—taking care of your baby. And the shit they pull when you are not looking. I failed to take into consideration the debilitating nature and exhaustion that comes with a ten-month-old's issues—namely separation anxiety when you want to hang out with your extended family for "summer camp." Gnocchi was unfamiliar with everyone and would barely let me pee without crying. We nicknamed her lulu lemons because it had gotten so bad that I began carrying her around like a sack of potatoes and because she was wearing a particularly cute jumpsuit with mini lemons on it when she got that nickname.

I thought she would be sleeping deeply at night to the soothing sounds of the forest animals and the last tweets of the birds saying goodnight. Instead, she was waking up at 2:00 am sweating from the electricity cutting.

Her schedule was off, and every time she looked out the window, I felt her look back at me as if to ask what had happened to all the buildings and why on earth they had been replaced with short stubby green things. I could only explain that those were "trees" so many times. I hoped it would make her stronger and the upside was that she got some quality time with her cousins who threatened to throw my phone in the pool (which they did) if I refused to let her consume any more lavender which I quickly found out causes diarrhea in infants.

Lovely.

So, we left Gnocchi with my parents for a few days, and we had to go just as my dad was getting out a huge jar of honey. That called for a simple laying down of what's safe and not safe. But of course, when it's your family, they aren't listening.

Here's what you say, and what they hear:

Me: No, Gnocchi can't have honey. She's not even a year old.
This is because honey can, occasionally, contain a spore of a bacterium called *Clostridium botulinum,* which can cause botulism (food

poisoning . . . I had to look it up, too) in babies. I do my research. According to health experts a child shouldn't have honey until after twelve months of age.

What they hear: "Of course I haven't given him honey yet because it's not fresh honey like from the all-natural beehive in your garden. So, yes, give him that honey . . . six months, eleven months, it's all really the same because the honey is, (say it with me now) FAAAA-RESH."

Me: "Gnocchi doesn't really like eggplant or tomatoes. So maybe you can feed her other stuff?"

What they hear: "I don't know how to cook or feed her eggplant or tomatoes the way she will like it, so please put her on a strict diet of those two items until she learns to love them because what half-Syrian, quarter-Palestinian, and quarter-Lebanese child doesn't love those two staples?"

Me: "Ice cream is just for special occasions."

What they hear: "Every day is a special occasion because they're with Teta and Jiddo (grandma and grandpa) so ice cream it is!"

Me: "No, don't cut anyone's hair, thanks."

What they hear: "I don't know how to cut her hair and haven't had time to do it myself or take her somewhere so please do me this favor."

I guess Gnocchi survived this parenting style—just as she and her little brothers seem to each time I leave them with their grandparents for a couple of days—and what doesn't kill them makes them stronger, right? Ummmm, except for the kebab and uncut apple they were convinced my third baby could eat with three teeth.

The point is that everything these foreign arms do—from that babysitter you stupidly found on Craigslist, to a live-in nanny (there's potential here for another book . . . except maybe I'll call it *The Helping Hand* which is catchier than *The Help*, right?) to your own parents—they do somewhat differently from the way we do it. From my parents to his parents (mostly his) even if it's done exactly the same way it is still not *our* way. I've compiled a list of false truths (if that's even what they're called). I spent roughly four months with my in-laws when Gnocchi was three months until she was seven months. In those months indispensable research was gathered rather unconsciously. And I would often rush to my room—my one safe haven in the entire apartment. This is not a direct attack on my in-laws because the same can be said about my parents' complete disregard for my rules and parenting style. The only difference is that I can yell at my parents and threaten not to visit anymore. Can I pull that same threat with my in-laws? I make my husband do it. Which he doesn't . . . so it all gets brushed under the carpet enough times until we are certain we all need a heavy helping of therapy. *Hi, my name is Sara and I have issues with my in-laws.* This is probably the best pick-up line in the world, but maybe we'll leave that for yet another book. *Finding the Magic in Your In-Laws.* Subtitle: *Live Far from Them.*

19

FILTER ON

(CONTROL+ALT+DELETE)

Let's fast-forward to almost month twelve when Gnocchi's brace gets removed. Yup, two weeks short of her first birthday. I was prepared to scream YIPPEE but was scared to celebrate it. Scared to begin buying her shorts and hesitant to enjoy the moment. Wanting to freeze and fast-forward both at the same time. But, you know what? The brace left our lives and we were all okay. It was all okay.

And then, you are facing a big milestone—the big 0-1. That's right. Your baby is done with her first year of mommyhood. You are done with your first year of mommyhood.

Let's go over all the big deals this entails. On the approach to the big 0-1 it's all about taking stock and measuring up how we did. Or is it just party planning? Your call.

The milestones. No one really cares about them but you. No, your baby doesn't, either. And neither will you a year or six months from now. And yet, in the moment it was *the* breaking news story of the decade to you and you are still confused as to why they didn't go viral. What do you mean Kanye West skydiving in a unicorn onesie was trending and not Gnocchi lifting her head? I couldn't believe she was lifting her head during tummy time. I snapped a photo and almost cried that she was no longer a newborn . . . but also realized that a thousand years ago, thousands of babies were doing the very same thing, that is—hitting the very same milestone and drooling. Except for back then, when a baby lifted her head, a goat was sacrificed. I don't remember when my second and third lifted their heads. I'm sure it was epic, but I'll just have to assume that it was.

The way you talk changed. Yes, in addition to your body and mindset, of course. Let's break this down a little more. Sure, you got married, fought a bit, made up (in whatever way) and then had a baby. But, all of a sudden everything becomes baby this and honey this and aww little baby coo-coo-poop-a-loo and your vocabulary changes. No, not just your intonation, but your actual words, too. Dog becomes doggy. Cat becomes kitty-witty. The problem is that there's no "off" button and you'll find yourself in a three-Michelin-star restaurant opposite your husband both dressed to the nines and smelling great (yes, showers taken) yet asking the waiter, "Can I have the ducky, pwease?"

Your goofs come back like a bad flashback. You consider what you did well and are doing well and what you completely failed at, like when she was three months old and I was *sure* she had her first tooth. I kept talking about what a typical Virgo and overachiever she was. Anyways, so here she was with a tooth, only it wasn't. It was a piece of banana. That was my first and far from last time I experienced a #parentingfail. Feeding her hummus . . . the list goes on.

You caught a bad case of *momnesia*. Like a fairy godmother's tap of a wand—just like that, we forget the burning smell, the contractions, and the catheter. We forget how much pain we were in and couple that with that moment where you tap your finger on your head and mutter "think woman, think" followed by "UGHHHH WHAT DID I COME IN TO GET. SHITTTT."

Congrats, you're a mama.

Good job for remembering to take your phone out of your back pocket before peeing today. Score! The hysterical moments. One day, you'll laugh about the time you left the vitamin D bottle near her and she drank half of it. Remember how you frantically googled "vitamin D overdose?" Well, that is until your older sister and mom woke up and began responding to all thirty-nine frantic messages you sent them between 4:00 and 4:05 a.m. Good times.

Along with the *momnesia* comes the "PA announcement syndrome"—why do mothers adopt the habit of saying out loud what they're leaving the room for, every time they leave the room? I blame it on developmental advice that encourages you to "talk to your baby" and "describe all surroundings." Sure, that's great and very educationally cute for a six month old, but is it still cute when your baby is a sixteen year old? Ummm, not so much. I caught myself telling my husband "Now, mommy is going to peeeee," when it was just the two of us at dinner. Long gone was the girl who used to brush her hand along his back, murmuring in his ear "Back in a sec …" and saunter off to the bathroom.

The most accurate way to measure how much your memory has been screwed by pregnancy (rather than ageing, alcohol, or a rather unfortunate head injury) is to read a book about pregnancy and see how much you can remember of it once you have a six-year-old. I can really only remember two things from all the parenting books I've ever read: "If you feel the urge to shake the baby—leave the room" and "Sleep when the baby sleeps." I mean, it's a good thing that I remembered to watch out for any violent urge. But "Sleep when baby sleeps"? Nobody does that, do they?

The over-bravoing. *Bravo* is a word I never thought I would use this much. It's understandable because I suppose everything and anything my daughter does is new and nothing short of a holy miracle. However, habits are formed as a result of lack of sleep and repetition. And so, my husband has often given me blank stares as a result of me shouting BRAVO and clapping my hands in his face after he has remembered to hang his towel up and not throw the damp towel on the bed. Quite an achievement and very well deserving of a high-pitched and passionate bravo, don't you think? Yes, I completely agree.

I hope you kept learning new stuff . . . I was never part of a sorority. I went to college, but in Beirut and Nottingham, thus I was robbed (spared?) of the beer guzzling and chanting of alpha beta catcha. Motherhood has given me that false sense of sisterhood, though. It is one big hive mind. This sorority of motherhood brings with it the continued education: thinking about things you never used to think about. Sharp corners, food allergies, temperature of potato wedges, and packing a blanket and a sweater everywhere you go. You tend to help anotha' motha' out when you see the chance. Conversations also change and soon you can barely talk about anything that doesn't revolve around naps, feeding, or the merits of letting your baby "cry it out." And so I urge you (mostly because I didn't) to make even the tiniest effort to cultivate interest in subjects outside of the boring talk of babies so you remain the cool person you were.

Mama Milestones

Unfortunately, moms don't get milestones to meet each month. We don't get measured and weighed and hugged and passed a balloon sticker and a lollipop when leaving the pediatrician's office. I mean, what mom wouldn't want to know how much faster she's gotten at changing her baby's diaper in a public bathroom? I would have loved nothing more to have my times recorded. Especially when she was still in that harness. Here are some mama milestones (twenty-four because I'm symbolic like that) that I would bet money you've by now achieved:

1. The number of minutes you're able to hang out with a floppy newborn until you reach for your phone is the same number of minutes it takes you to pour a glass of water.

2. Your definition of a successful day comes down to being able to feed and burp before the end of an entire season of your latest Netflix binge.

3. You have perfected the ability to speak exclusively high-pitched nonsense for over ten minutes.

4. Mastered how to make drooling look elegant.

5. Made dinner plans guilt-free. Okay, with the guilt.

6. Had a twenty-minute one-sided conversation about their stuffed bunny. And for some reason that bunny always has diarrhea because it's sure to get a giggle.

7. Any song by Ed Sheeran makes you sob. Also, Michael Jackson. Oh, and the theme song to *Sesame Street*. Basically, anything that isn't dance music. And sometimes, even dance music.

8. You never could look at your gynecologist the same way after birth. That's why you had to find a new one for your pap smears because that person saw your ugly cry go on for hours and hours.

9. Your "big deal scale" changed. You either pushed something out of your vagina or were cut open, so while getting fired was not a biggie, needing any other medical intervention—even filling a cavity— is cause for that groundswell of vulnerability. This extends to cutting your baby's fingernails. Some of us … Just. Can't. Go. There.

10. You've attempted a 5 p.m. bedtime only to have remembered that a 5 p.m. bedtime means a 4 a.m. wake up call. No, thanks.
11. Spoken to your six-month-old as an adult with extra emphasis on each syllable. Ex: "I don't understand what you WANTTT," when you're really about to lose it.
12. Mixed up the names of your child's stuffed animals and then apologized believably.
13. Gone outside into the garden at 5 a.m. (when your baby has woken up for no apparent reason) closed your eyes with your child on your lap and described things you're "seeing" in the garden. "Look baby . . . there's a bee . . . and a bird . . . and, oh, wow . . . is that a tiger?"
14. Been annoyed at those moms who claim that their two-year-old doesn't "H-I-T."
15. Been excited when there's a free talk at a children's clothing store nearby because free talk = free cookies and unlimited bitching. And that provides a great setting for new friendships to thrive.
16. Woken up and immediately felt exhausted. It's called *Yamflnran*—you're a mama for life. No running away now.
17. Your own saliva has been used as a disinfectant and stain remover.
18. Peed and pulled up without wiping in order to stop your toddler from drinking shampoo or spraying something in their eye.
19. Scooped up vomit with your bare hands and be called a hero for it.
20. Caught floating poop in your hands, you know, to stop it floating around during bath time.
21. Lied and said that you have an "emergency" to cut to the front of a bathroom or coffee line.
22. Scraped at some sort of dried up discoloration and sniff it to figure out if it's puke or milk or yogurt. Yes, you tasted it, too. Not that it would matter but somehow it just does.
23. Cried when hugging your mom good morning because you get it now.
24. Fell asleep facedown in something.

Future You?

And now, onto a "future-you" quiz as my final quiz, mama. This one tells you what kind of mama you will be for your toddler. Even if you're already sure, go ahead and double check. It's always better to be safe than sorry, remember? Isn't that why we always pack extra packets of raisins? This one doesn't have multiple choice questions, you'll just know which mama you are by that sinking feeling in your gut when you read it.

Let's imagine you're at the playground and your baby is a little older. You're a little older. You're into that negotiating phase of parenting. If you're anything like me, the playground is wonderful—for all of five minutes for me, and forever for her. I'm always immediately looking for ways to get mine to go home. I've looked around for moms to model off of, and this is what I see:

1. The Lifestyle Mommy: This mommy likes to leave with her dignity (and her daughter's) dignity intact. No empty threats here, as she believes in keeping the peace and life being all about peace, love, and happiness. She's composing her next beautiful Insta-post, anyway. She will let her child play an extra forty-five minutes because she's barely watching and who cares if she has to reschedule her doctor's appointment again. Not a biggie. She knows that she has bigger battles ahead when she dishes up zucchini soup for dinner or gets sued by her kid in fifteen years for breach of privacy. Key mantra: Don't look now, I'm expanding my platform and featuring you in my next blog.

2. The Negotiator: "If you leave I'll shower you in gifts and cold hard cash. Promise." The negotiator has a schedule to stick to and is vocal about her strategy and distraction tactics in the hopes that their child's advanced (she would never use the word "limited") sense of reason kicks in and they realize that a bigger win is around the corner. She has tricks up her sleeves, snacks in her pockets, and dangles educational Apps to lure. "Guess who has your favorite pasta dish with melted cheese . . . yeah . . . it's in the car . . . and there's an ice cream in my purse IF you come NOW!" Key mantra: Help me, help you. (flashback to Jerry Maguire)

3. The Victim: Can be overheard saying, "Don't you think Mommy is tired?" She voices why and how her back, head and (insert any body part here) hurts or feels as if her toddler is actually her osteopath. She is prone to floods of tears and eventually her kid stares at her with, "I wish mommy would just pop an Advil or six and get her s@#! together," in their eyes. Key mantra: What about meeee?

4. The Truster in the Universe: She is wise. And just. And calmer than the lifestyle mommy who is really only cool as a cucumber for the credit of being labeled an "amazing parent." She knows (somehow . . . either because she believes in God or because this is her fourth or fifth child) that THIS, whatever THIS is, in the moment is really not a big deal. So what if they want to swing for another ten minutes or fifty? It is not the end of the world. She has freezer meals at the ready back home, anyway. But not saying grace/bedtime affirmations/kiddie meditation, though, that's another story. Key mantra: This too shall pass.

5. The Dictator: "I'm leaving with or without you. Good-bye!" No negotiations or five more minutes here. Usually hyped up from too much caffeine and too little sleep (my husband strangely seems to think I fall into this category) she is skilled in the nonchalant grab-and-go technique. Key mantra: I'm the boss, get into the car or I will lose it completely.

Whichever of these archetypes rings a bell, don't judge yourself too harshly, the truth is, getting your child to leave is FRUSTRATING and sometimes it's better to let them swing a few more minutes, you know, to save yourself a therapy bill later on. Some may call me a pushover but I consider myself a truster in the universe. And a negotiator and, yes, a dictator when I haven't slept enough.

*Please note that the personas depicted in this piece are in no way exaggerated and if you come to my park you will see a display of every single one. When are you coming? No, seriously, when's your flight arriving?

Let Them Eat Cake (And You Should, Too)

The votes are in. You lose a lot and you gain a lot. What's the scorecard, though? In motherhood there are so many things that are forever lost. Your pre-pregnancy body, your ability to remember simple things, and that one thing you swear you used to have . . . and, no, I'm not talking about your willingness to wear heels. I'm talking about your patience. You know, that quality you pray for more of and promise you're going to dish out in vast quantities tomorrow morning.

I am still amazed when watching magic (even the simple kids' party standard of magic where the twenty-something-year-old fumbles through half the tricks). It is this optimistic quality that sees me excited to wake up every morning even on three hours of sleep. We are all like this as kids. We high five our sibling at the notion of getting to stay up an extra thirty minutes and giggle at being allowed to sleep in our bathing suit and flippers because we have succeeded in convincing our mom that we have an underwater rescue mission to save a lost dolphin. We laugh uncontrollably when someone threatens to "catch us" after "eating our nose." As adults we hope these games have in no way influenced our running from commitment and wanting to get a nose job to have a nose that we would like people to want to eat.

So many books and articles have been written about this whole mommyhood thing. So many speeches given and knowing glances handed out like flyers for complimentary facials. The information might not be new, but I've tried to give the packaging and overall message a fresh spin. Yeah, we pee, and puke, and think *ohmygod I'm growing a person*, and hate on our MIL, and all that. All that is expected. What isn't expected is the armor we sprout. It's self-polishing. The armor we keep on and cherish to trudge through the trenches of the hard bits and find that magic. That metallic armor is what we need to let the light bounce off of. We think it's magic but it's really us getting through the muddy bits and quicksand and making it to the other side.

I still ask myself those questions: Am I a good mom? Am I spending enough time with her? Am I spending too much time with her? When is it okay to call your friends' kid nicknames? "Sweet puppy little cookascoop" sounds better than Hani, sure, but is one playdate in too soon to be handing out nicknames? But, I now know I won't always know the answer, so I've narrowed down my entire philosophy in motherhood to be the following: *Cracks are what let the light through* and *Let them eat cake*. The first just to keep perspective and positive mind and the second because a child is a child once. But, yes, that cake better damn well be gluten-free and vegan and every sort of free. Kinda, but not really, because then it's not cake.

So, I believe in the magic. Call me stupid, but I do. It's not handed over and, yeah, we have to look for it and usually struggle to find it, but it's there outside of the clichés and expectations and far away from any judgment. I'm not one to fix things and so I'm not going to be the fixer here, either, and solve anything for you. The males in our life are there for that solution-oriented speak. I'm just here to steal a line from *Ghost* and say "Ditto."

I've done that, too.

I say let them eat cake and let the mama have her ugly cry and I'll have one along with her. No meme-able joke, or Insta-ready quotes to post. Just some candid girl-talk. Some real hiccup-venting and currency-hunting. We don't have to say we're all a hot mess and we don't have to paint this perfect life, either. This Goldilocks is looking for the mamas that are just right. Just themselves. Just exactly who they are as mamas. Nothing else.

This was never going to be a book of advice or guidelines for the perfect way forward. Instead, it's a reminder to pause and laugh to help you through the chaos. This is a book about making it through to turning the big 0-1. It's really about finding the magic, yes, and knowing that a part of it is when you think you can't hold your breath anymore to find that you actually can and the breath you suck in (when you can) is that much sweeter. It's when you've hit rock-bottom to realize there's a worse situation waiting for you and then you come back up. It's having a silly filter on and calling it for what it is—ridiculous and semi-forced but, hey, at least you're being you.

Funnily enough, in a few years all of this pain and suffering (a bit melodramatic, so sorry, but I'm tired, too) will be nothing more than a distant memory for the sole reason that when someone asks you what it's like in the beginning you can confidently shrug and say, "Ohhhh, you'll get through it . . . it's really not that bad."

There's nothing like a mama's love, though. I get it now. And there can't be because something is put inside us to wipe the poop, scoop up the puke, and stay up all night checking fevers with minimal complaining except when ordering that extra espresso shot.

I want to tell you about the lizards and love bugs before I go. Yeah. I am wrapping this sucker up. But we're still besties, right?

We used to play this one game to torture my mom and get her to prove her love for us called lizards and love bugs. Okay, so I just tried to make the game sound much cooler than it was. It didn't even have a name, but it was a bit like Would You Rather? So, the game is pretty self-explanatory. We created it and by we, I mean my older brother. It was all about what she would do to save us from getting shot/locked up forever/cutting off one of our toes and other gruesome and disturbing scenarios. We would ask her stuff like what if someone walked up to you and told you that you had to boil up a few rats and pigeons and eat up five bowls of that stew with sprinkled cockroaches in one sitting or they would kidnap us and you wouldn't see us for fifteen years. What would you do mama? Huh? She would respond with a calm and collected, "Eat up the stew, obviously," right? Good mama. Disgusting, yes, but still totally the right answer here.

But what if someone said they would scratch our eyes out (it got gruesome at times, which totally makes sense now since you know my brother ended up being a surgeon) unless you ate the arm hairs of fifty strange men and a few eyeballs, what would you do? The answer was clear. But after playing this for four hours straight on a long car ride where my dad refused to ask for directions, her answers drastically shifted.

She became so fed up with our scenarios (or my Daddy's driving) that she opted for the "wrong" answers, to which we would shout, "Mammmmaaaaa!" In shock. How could she? Of course, she'd rather eat the bug stew than let us go toeless. Wouldn't she? If she chose the disgusting option over us, which involved anything from cockroaches to boogers and rat poop, we were disappointed and betrayed. And if she chose having someone shave our heads and ship us off to Mexico where she wouldn't see us for a year then we were even more hurt. It was a lose-lose situation. We knew deep down inside that she would do it. She would jump and eat and steal and break and swallow if that meant she was keeping us safe.

What we were doing to her was unreasonable, of course, but that's parenting. It's all unreasonable and just a little bit crazy. True mental combat.

The best thing my mom has ever done for me (I mean, besides playing that stupid game for hours), was give me permission. To doubt. To question. To fear. As a mom, there are certain things you can never learn. Certain things that can't be bought or taught or understood. You just have to accept and hope that the unpleasantness or uncertainty will pass. But, still, we learn to look these fears straight in the eye then call our moms or trusted Aunty J and ask if what we are feeling is normal before bursting into tears and digging a spoon deep into a carton of macadamia nut brittle (that's my go-to flavor for quieting trepidation).

Moms make mistakes.

I make tons. Wrong snack. Not enough blankets, too many blankets. Posing as a helicopter mom in music class or too uninvolved in her dance class. It's hard and the clichés make it harder. Every uterus is unique, yes, and every roadmap to finding that glimpse of magic or glimmer of hope takes a different route. It's where we spend our mama currency that gets us through it. Now, let's hold hands and sing "Kumbaya." Of course, you can chime in with that drum.

I constantly feel selfish and guilty and generally exhausted, so, congrats to me. I am officially a mom in those moments and every other. Dare I say, a damn good one, too? *Always* according to my mama and *never* according to my in-laws. It is a place where you will see yourself scramble to offer up anything from ice cream to your car keys . . . and the car . . . and letting them actually drive a bit if that's what it takes to stop their extended whining. And so why can't we try to be these mamas who aren't afraid of showing their real Instastory, who can laugh at our mess-ups, and then sob, "It all went by too fast."

And here's where I tell you to turn the page for the Mommyfesto. Call me up. Let's bitch a bit and vent and sob together. Ummm, actually, I'd rather not give out my number so DM me on social. And I'll tell myself patience young grasshopper patience and continue tweeting. Until then, I guess I'm going to be ordering another espresso and calling my mom.

The Real Reason We All Have Kids

And before I knew it, Gnocchi was slowly growing into a mini version of me. Like a caterpillar into a butterfly, except she was much more gorgeous than a caterpillar and antennae-free and I was far from a butterfly although my mom would argue that one. Thanks for the ego boost, mommy. She was changing, though. Changing into a better version of me, but a slice of me, still. She was like that pink plastic wedge to fit into that Trivial Pursuit pie when you get the answer right. Here was this little girl who hated her hair, occasionally bit her cuticles in excitement, and loved listening to African beats and had the dance moves to prove it. Her love of all things silly and carefree ability to laugh easily while still being a perfectionist is what made me understand why people would try and do this whole thing again. And again. And this time I would try and remember to remind myself that the the gap between our expectations and the reality, is where we find the magic of mommyhood.

MOMMYFESTO

YOU ARE A MOM.
EMBRACE IT.

YOU WILL NEVER SNOOZE AGAIN. VALUE CATNAPS. TRUST YOUR GUT. IF YOU FEEL LIKE YOU HAVE NO IDEA WHAT YOU'RE DOING, FAKE IT. REMEMBER YOUR KIDS ARE PEOPLE – EASILY MOLDED AND EASILY BROKEN. **LET THEM SEE THE MAGIC** IN EVERYTHING. YOU WILL MAKE MISTAKES. YOU CAN HANDLE ANYTHING. YOU JUST HAVE TO FIGURE OUT HOW. BE GRATEFUL. **IF YOU ARE NOT A MORNING PERSON CHANGE.** IF YOU ARE UNHAPPY WITH HOW TIRED YOU ALWAYS FEEL, **ORDER ANOTHER ESPRESSO.** IF YOU FEEL OVERWHELMED BY IT ALL, **CALL YOUR MOM. HELP THEM WIPE, REACH AND DREAM.** SHOW THEM THINGS YOU LOVE, PROTECT THEM FROM THINGS YOU FEAR. ACCEPT THAT THEY ARE INDIVIDUALS WHO WILL LOVE AND FEAR DIFFERENT THINGS. HUG OFTEN; **CUDDLES ARE LIFE'S MARSHMALLOWS.** MAKE THINGS WITH YOUR HANDS. SHARE SECRETS EVEN IF THEY ARE TOO YOUNG TO UNDERSTAND. THE BEST AGE IS THE AGE YOUR KIDS ARE RIGHT NOW. DO NOT SPEND TOO MUCH TIME WISHING, HOPING OR REGRETTING. SET AN EXAMPLE. IMPERFECTION IS PART OF PERFECTION. **GIGGLES ARE GOLDEN.** YOU WILL FEEL LIKE YOU'RE DOING A GOOD JOB FOR 3 SECONDS EVERY MONTH. SHAKE OFF JUDGMENT. CRY, HUG, REPEAT. WHEN IT RAINS LOOK FOR RAINBOWS. PAY ATTENTION TO SMILES, NOT STAINS. MAKE UP WORDS TO SONGS. **BE SILLY. STOP AND NOTICE IT ALL.** DON'T EXPECT A PERFECT DAY. IT'S NOT A RACE, UNLESS IT IS. FORGIVE YOURSELF FOR MAKING MISTAKES. INTENTIONS MATTER MORE. ENJOY THE SPILLS, CRUMBS, AND TEARS. IT IS ALL JUST A PASSING MOMENT. **TEACH THEM ALL ABOUT LIFE. LEARN FROM THEM WHAT LIFE IS ALL ABOUT.**

All words belong to me but the formatting for my mommyfesto comes from The Holstee Manifesto. See more at www.holstee.com.

CHARTS

(ALL ILLUSTRATIONS BY MOI, WITH COLORING CONTRIBUTIONS FROM ONE OF MY LITTLE PUZZLE PIECES, ADRIANA)

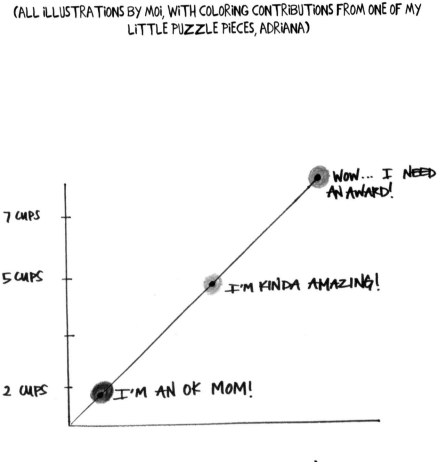

HOW COFFEE AFFECTS MOTHERHOOD

The idea of the charts was "copied like an artist" from @instachaaz. Check him out!

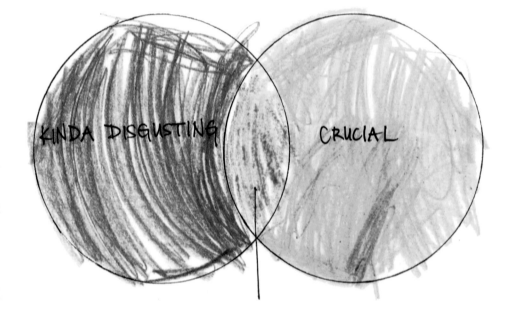

KINDA DISGUSTING   CRUCIAL

PICKING MY KIDS NOSE

PARENTS WHO TRY
TO SLEEP TRAIN THEIR
KIDS

PARENTS WHO SUCCEED
IN SLEEP TRAINING

A LOT OF COUNTING 1—3

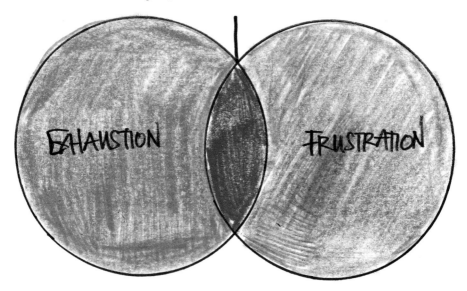

EXHAUSTION

FRUSTRATION

THINGS I VALUE AT 6

AM

COFFEE

IF ITS OBVIOUS
MY MASCARA IS
FROM THE NIGHT BEFORE

PM

WINE

IF I HAVE TO SHAVE
FOR TONIGHTS DINNER

WHAT KIDS PLAY WITH

A

B

A: STORE BOUGHT EXPENSIVE TOYS
B: HAIR CLIPS, WRAPPING PAPER, EMPTY PLASTIC BOTTLES

INTEREST IN WRITING IN THE BABY JOURNAL

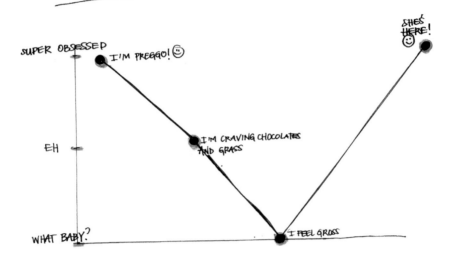

SUPER OBSESSED — I'M PREGGO! ☺

EH

WHAT BABY?

I'M CRAVING CHOCOLATES AND GRASS

I FEEL GROSS

SHE'S HERE! ☺

SCALE OF ANNOYANCE

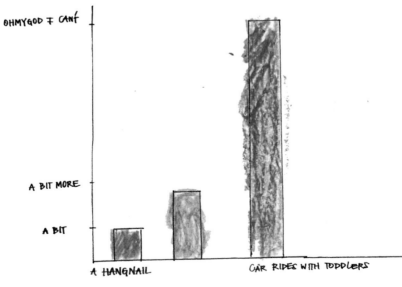

OHMYGOD I CAN'T

A BIT MORE

A BIT

A HANGNAIL

MISSING A FLIGHT

CAR RIDES WITH TODDLERS

WHAT YOU DO WHEN THE BABY'S SLEEPING

1. MAKE LISTS OF WHAT YOU HAVE TO DO
2. UNDERLINE AND HIGHLIGHT
3. YAWN, GET IN PJ'S AND JUSTIFY NAP
4. PANIC ABOUT HOW YOU SHOULD BE MORE EFFICIENT
5. REARRANGE CLOSET
6. SCROLL THROUGH INSTAGRAM
7. NOW FACEBOOK
8. LOOK AT WHATS AP MESSAGES
9. LOOK AT BLACK BAGS ONLINE AND IN MIRROR
10. GO PICK UP CRYING BABY AND APPLAUD YOURSELF FOR GETTING SO MUCH DONE IN 35 MINS.

ABOUT THE AUTHOR

Sara Sadik, a Palestinian Lebanese energetic mom of three puzzle pieces delivers her distinct brand of warm candid humor with an extra dose of sass in a traditional Arabic coffee cup. A Post-it/highlighter/notebook aficionado who tries to always tell it like it is, her secret sauce is finding humor in any situation and she's on a mission to make you see the lighter side, breathe, and know you're not alone in this unpredictable odyssey through mommyhood.

Sara is married to American-born Syrian, Mr. Excel, whose career in Private Equity finances her Starbucks triple-shot soy cappuccinos. Together, they're thirtysomethings who used to skydive and go on safaris for kicks, but now enjoy looking for stuffed bunnies and superman Band-Aids.

With a Palestinian dad and a Lebanese mom, Sara's lived on three continents, in five countries, and muses on how moms-to-be and moms-in-action think, feel, question, and seek magic in their lives—regardless of location: from Delaware to Dubai, where she has lived for the past seven years. She reads to her kids on most nights (usually *I Love You, Stinky Face* by Lisa McCourt) but never skips a morning dance-off (usually Shakira or Mumford & Sons).

A big believer in pinkie promises, peanut butter for protein, and, no surprise—magic, Sara will have coffee with anyone for the chance to vent about mothers-in-law and share in a good ol' fashioned sob fest. A kid at heart, Sara knows every single word to every single Disney song (a task she accomplished before having kids) and enjoys snacking on free samples of anything.

She has previously worked for the *Daily Star* newspaper, the United Nations, and the prime minister's office in Dubai until they realized that her creativity and dance moves were unproductive. Or so she tells herself.

Sara created her brand, *Finding the Magic in Mommyhood* because she acknowledges that not all moments in mommyhood (and in life, really) are entirely magical. Despite being an optimist at heart, she realized that parenting was much more than being happy-go-lucky and much more like hey-it's-okay-to-have-hard-bits. Let's hold hands, cry about it, and look for that damn rainbow.

GLOSSARY OF TERMS

Aloo Gobi

One of my many Indian cravings with my first, little gnocchi. Cauliflower with potatoes sautéed with turmeric, curry leaves, and spice. *A lotta* spice.

Breggo

Preggo but in the Arabic language there is no P letter or sound and so words beginning with P are spelled and pronounced as B. BANCAKES, BOOL, and, yes, my all-time favorite: BEBSI.

BPPM

Big Psycho Pregnancy Moment. All I remember is that mine involved some sort of a food . . . or song. Or maybe Mr. Excel was just breathing too close to me.

Coosa bi Laban

The Arab version of mac and cheese comfort food. Zucchini stuffed with rice and minced meat in yogurt sauce.

DDH

Hip Dysplasia is often referred to as Developmental Dysplasia of the Hip or DDH. It is generally the preferred term for babies and children with hip dysplasia since this condition can develop after birth.

DM

Direct Messaging. Acronyms just make us sound cooler and more knowledgeable about what we're talking about because essentially, we're just cutting out two syllables so acronyms are not for saving time, really, are they?

Habibti

My darling or my one who is loved. If I was a boy she would've called me *Habibi* but I wasn't so she didn't.

Jiddo

Grandfather.

Mabrook

A celebratory congratulation that is sometimes used sarcastically. It is also always overused. "*Mabrook*, you found a good parking spot." Or "*Mabrook*, you learned how to boil the right amount of spaghetti."

Meghli

Meghli is a traditional Lebanese dessert that is served to celebrate the birth of a baby. It is a delicious rice pudding spiced with anise, cinnamon, and caraway and garnished with shredded coconut and nuts. Kinda like Vegemite in that you either love it or hate it. It does help with the production of breast milk, though.

Oo iza

Loosely translated to mean, "so what?" or "who cares?" Example: You met Beyoncé and Ed Sheeran and had dinner with them? (Proceed to swallow your intense jealously.) *Oo iza.* This is also said to show you completely couldn't care less about something when it's really killing you inside.

Teta

Grandmother. Grandma or Grandmama if you want to be really annoying.

Warak Enab

A Lebanese dish of grape leaves stuffed with spiced rice and beef and simmered in a lemony broth. Oh, and my mama's is better than yours.

Yalla, Yallah, or Yala

Probably the most commonly used expression in Arabic. It means let's go, hurry up, move your ass, or most typically a combination of all three. It is no surprise that my children's first words have been daddy, *bebe,* (baby) and *yalla.* So much for letting kids take their time.

Ya omri

Exactly translated it means "my life" as a word, but hang on, it can get confusing. There is more than that one use. For example, when you want to tell someone about your age you can say, "*omri* twenty-nine" which means "my age is twenty-nine." But, in this case my teta was talking about "her life or baby" or whatever and nothing to do with her age or mine. And yes, I am twenty-nine. Yup. Anyways, tangent and mini Arabic lesson over.

Ya rouhi

You are my soul or my dear beloved. It's all a little melodramatic and endearing as is most of the Arabic language. Words of endearment involve honey, soul, life, and breath of fresh air (could be making that last one up). Maybe that's why it's so difficult to learn and also why we tend to be so emotionally draining?

ACKNOWLEDGMENTS

Adsi, Rio, and Rambo—thank you for teaching me all about perseverance, the beauty of non-conformity, and the importance of charm.

To my parents, thank you for teaching me to love even the smell of books and how to take everything in life "bird by bird."

Mr. Excel, it's always been you. From Irish Spring to Molton Brown, thank you for always reminding me to keep things in perspective and waiting so patiently until my moments of psychosis passed.

Karim and Mira, thank you for dealing with my self-doubt and self-pity the only way an older brother and sister would, with just the right amount of tactful tough love to make me get over it.

Lizzie, thank you for helping me turn my book crumbs into something, but, mostly, for holding my hand through it all. There is no doubt that your pom-poms and "chu-can-do-its" got me here.

Katsu, your words stuck with me. "Make friends with uncertainty and learn to love incomplete things until they are complete."

Aunty J (Jen), only a girl from Baltimore could stop me from over-thinking, second-guessing, and start looking at my problems as luxuries.

Diana, you saw the magic in this little idea when no other agent could.

Mr. Langholz, you nurtured my enthusiasm as a nine-year old without knowing if what you taught me would stick and turn into something unexpected like this.

To Nicole, thank you for putting up with my 5,001 emails at all hours of the night and for polishing it up for me without deleting my swear words and diluting my edge.

To all my girlfriends around the world—from Bogotá, Beirut, Grand-Baie, NYC, DC, Miami, and, of course, Dubai—here's to always laughing through the hard bits. Oh, and to always fakin' it until we make it. To those with kids and those without, those who live near me and those who are miles away, thank you for always laughing at all my lame jokes and calling me out when it wasn't funny. I love you guys for making me think I had it in me all along.

To Natski, Mouse, and Goat, thanks for always bringing out the "craxi" colorful imagination in me and going along with my fabricated stories that always end in exciting adventures . . . and just enough trouble.

To Poulet, Slothy, Tifa, and Pilarita, I wanted to wear my Marymount uniform and pose for the front cover but the publisher shot that idea down fast. Thanks for always being my friend when I had braces, awkward dance moves (yeah, I know I still do), and short MJ pants.

To Bis, Mish, Pammy, Josephina, Hawky, and GQ—my time in NYC wouldn't have been the same or even a fraction as fun without you guys. Or without those popkas.

To Thubsi, D, and AvaJan—I'm forever thankful for the communal playdates so I could escape for a bit and write and rewrite but mostly question what I was doing.

To Twentymazing Riham, for reminding me that I was more than a mom. At least on some nights.

Mark Manson for reminding us that reading could be edgy.

Dr. Zakieh Al Jayousi, thank you for always giving medical advice like only a mama would and for reminding me that every fever and rash would soon pass but mostly that the brace wouldn't stay on forever.